EURIPIDES
MEDEA

Also by DESMOND EGAN

Poetry

Midland (1972)
Leaves (1974)
Siege! (1977)
Woodcutter (1978)
Athlone? (1980)
Seeing Double (1983)
Snapdragon (1983, 1991)
Poems for Peace (1986)
A Song For My Father (1989)
Peninsula (1991)

Collected Poems (1983, 1984)
Selected Poems (Edited by Hugh Kenner) (1991)

In Translation

Terre et Paix (French/English) (1988)
Echobogen (Dutch/English) (1990)

Prose

The Death of Metaphor Selected Prose (1990)

Critical Study

Desmond Egan: The Poet and His Work
(Edited by Hugh Kenner, U.S.A. 1990)

EURIPIDES
MEDEA

translated by
DESMOND EGAN

with an Introduction by
Brian Arkins

— 1991 —

 ST. ANDREWS PRESS U.S.A.
KAVANAGH PRESS IRELAND

Published by
THE ST. ANDREWS PRESS Inc.
St. Andrews College, Laurinburg, North Carolina 28352
THE KAVANAGH PRESS Ltd.
Newbridge, Co. Kildare, Ireland

First Edition 1991
Printed in Great Britain
ISBN 0-032662-90-4 St. Andrews Press
ISBN 1-870491-26-2 Kavanagh Press

Front cover: Tom Sperling (U.S.A.)

ACKNOWLEDGEMENTS

This book is in part made possible by a generous grant from
The Hanes Charitable Lead Trust.

The translator wishes to acknowledge with gratitude the
encouragement and help he consistently received on this project from
Dr. Brian Arkins, Department of Classics, University College, Galway.

Back Cover quotation from *Thucydides and Lough Owel - The
Greek Connection* by Brian Arkins, in 'Desmond Egan, The Poet and His
Work' edited by Hugh Kenner (U.S.A. 1990).

Made and printed in Great Britain by
The Guernsey Press Co. Ltd., Guernsey, Channel Islands.

For
Michael Sundermeier
and the Staff and Students of
Creighton University, Omaha

and for
Brian Arkins
the onelie begetter

CONTENTS

INTRODUCTION

Brian Arkins*

SEVERAL texts from the Greco-Roman past cry out for a feminist reading - Plato's *Symposiuum*, Cicero's speech *In Defence of Ceelius*, Ovid's *Amores* - but none has a better claim than Euripides' great play *Medea*, first performed in Athens in 431 B.C.

1.

During the 5th century B.C. in the city-state - or *polis* - of Athens, civilization reached heights that were rarely, if ever, to be paralleled in history; as Yeats said,

> Civilization rose to its high-tide mark in Greece, fell, rose again in the Renaissance but not to the same level. (1)

We have the creation of history by the two very different personalities of the omnivorous Herodotus and the essentially political Thucydides; the astonishing development of philosophy both by the Sophists and by Socrates (with Plato and Aristotle to follow); the magnificent sculpture and architecture, especially as seen in the buildings on the Acropolis; the hilariously funny comedies of Aristophanes; and, by no means least, the great tragedies of Aeschylus, Sophocles and Euripides. An achievement

*Brian Arkins is statutory lecturer in Classics, University College, Galway; a distinguished Classical Scholar, he is author of a book on Catullus and of 'Builders Of My Soul: Greek and Roman Themes in the Poetry of W. B. Yeats.' Dr. Arkins has recently completed, for publication in U.S.A., a book-length study of the poetry of Desmond Egan.

which not only exists in its own right, but which has radically affected us all; as Desmond Egan has said,

> We are all Greeks - in the way we think, in the language we use, in literature, in drama, in ethics, in sport, in politics in science, in medicine, in architecture. (2)

But the astounding achievements took place against a severely troubled background (3): Athens, with the rest of Greece, had to ward off a Persian invasion; Athens then, within a few decades, built an Empire and lost it, defeated by Sparta in the cataclysmic Peloponnesian War; and, all the while, Athens was a city conducting within itself great debates about the meaning of life and death, about politics, religion, ethics - in modern terms deconstructing the achievement as it unfolded. The greatest of these debates concerned the respective claims in human life of the polarities - the binary opposition - of nature (*physis*) and of law, custom, practice (*nomos*): were certain things so because nature ordained them, or were they merely human inventions, alterable at will? A debate very pertinent to Euripides' *Medea*.

Euripides is certainly, together with Thucydides and Aristophanes, one of the central chroniclers of 5th century disruption. As Euripides raises questions about the role of war in *The Trojan Women*, about ecstatic religion in the *Bacchae*, about sexual love in the *Hippolytus*, about the position of women in *Medea*, he shows us that, in Greek terms, there is no order *(kosmos)* in the world as we experience it, presided over by beneficent gods, but rather the opposite, disorder (*khaos*), presided-over by gods who are at best indifferent and at worst actively hostile.

2.

It was, presumably, inevitable that among the great debates there should surface that concerning one of the central binary oppositions which human beings contend with, that between women and men. But before we look at how Euripides handles this, we must consider the actual position of women in 5th century Athens.

Just as a Marxist struggle to come to terms with the Athenian achievement - with how it must, as Marx held,

> count as a norm and as an unattainable model. (4)

although based on slave labour - so must a feminist reckon with the fact that women were almost totally excluded from the great political and cultural happenings in 5th century Athens. By contrast, aristocratic women in Rome during the late Republic and early Empire - the first centuries B.C. and A.D. - were far more free, able to walk about the city easily, to attend games, to go to dinner-parties, to initiate divorce proceedings and retain their own property after divorce. But the aristocratic woman in 5th century Athens could do none of these things and was, almost literally, confined to the house. For the house (*oikos*) was the woman's domain, her space, as the city (*polis*) was the man's.

Man worked in the fields, in the market the affairs of the city; women's work was spinning wool, baking and keeping house.

There is therefore a radical sundering between the worlds that men and women respectively inhabit, a sundering well caught by Marylin Arthur:

> The generalized orientation of the man is centrifugal, directed towards the outer world, the bright light of day; his activities concern the production and circulatio n of goods; and his code of behaviour is modelled on the agonistic (competitive) in the *agora* (market-place) - the world of challenge and *riposte*. By contrast, the female principle of movement is centripetal, oriented towards the shadowy inner recesses of the house; her work is reproduction and consumption, the activities which maintain life on a daily, cyclical basis: cooking and spinning, food and clothing; her code of behaviour requires indirectness of approach, face turned away, eyes cast downward; and she speaks the language of lies, secrets, and silence.(5)

However, this cosy male-imposed arrangement is, like everything else, subject to breakdown and, because the woman/man dichotomy is so central, the breakdown will result in a radical attack on the male-dominated *polis*. A situation regarded by the world of men as either a joke - women in comedy are often represented as mad for sex and drink - or as a nightmare - women in tragedy often subvert the established order.

In *Medea* it is definitely nightmare, what Medea does it to take on the male *polis* and on its own terms, and by vigorous, brutal, action attack its most cherished presumptions. Medea, in short, beats the men at their own game.

3.

Medea is, of course a play, not a social document (6). Equally, the ideology it deals with is that of 5th century Athens and specifically the position of women in that society. *Medea* can therefore be read in terms of binary oppositions, with the overriding opposition that between female and male, Medea and Jason.

Medea, who is the granddaughter of the Sun-God and skilled in poisons, comes from Colchis and there helps Jason to acquire the Golden Fleece. They fall in love, get married, return to Greece, and have two children. As the play begins, Jason abandons Medea in order to marry Glauke, daughter of the King of Corinth (where they live) and so provide himself with the security of marriage into a Greek royal family; as the Nurse says, literally, Jason,

> sleeps with a royal marriage.

It is important to understand that Jason enters into this new marriage, not for love of Glauke, but because she represents the security he craves. This is no eternal triangle in the modern sense, in fact it constitutes the reverse, for *Jason loved Medea, but just wishes to be married to Glauke.*

We can develop further the oppositions inherent in this intensely dramatic situation. Beneath the umbrella of the man/woman conflict there are the added polarities of custom (*nomos*) versus nature (*physis*); of city (*polis*) versus house (*oikos*); of marriage versus sexual love (*eros*); of Greek versus foreigner. In other words, Jason stands for the public world of the Greek city and its value-system, which stresses marriage; Medea, for the private world of the foreign person and her value-system, which stresses love.

As a foreigner, Medea is in a special position to demolish Jason's system and that is what she proceeds to do with devastating effect. Not only does she engineer the death of Glauke and of Glauke's father, King Creon, but she also, horrifically, kills her own two children, *and is then given sanctuary in Athens by King Aegeus, brought there from Corinth in the chariot of the Sun-God.* So this quadruple murderess is endorsed by the

Gods and the city of Athens - surely one of the most shocking statements ever made in the history of Athenian drama, something to send shivers down every male back during this very civic occasion in the Theatre of Dionysus, the God of Paradox; the reason, surely, why Euripides came last in the contest in 431 B.C. But also, as we can now see, the first major feminist statement in European literature and one of the greatest - for Medea is, precisely, a great woman.

4.

In his new translation, Desmond Egan, a major poet who knows Greek, has captured extremely well the text of Euripides which these introductory remarks have tried to delineate - as well, I should say, as is possible in English at this time. Egan avoids the twin traps that constitute Scylla and Charybdis for all translators: on the one hand, a translation which, by giving the letter, obscures and ruins the spirit of the original; on the other, a translation which is more a version, executed by a translator intent upon obtruding him/herself and preoccupations, into the original.

What we have here - and it is a rare phenomenon - is the genuine article: a translation that sticks rigorously to the original, but not in a way that presents ludicrous language of the type parodied by Housman. Indeed, Egan has followed the admirable precepts of another accomplished translation from the Greek, that of Richmond Lattimore who suggests that the translator,

> must use all his talents, his understanding of the language and of the meaning of the original and his own skill in verse, to make a new piece of verse-work which represents, to him, what the original would be, might be, or ought to be, must be ,in English. This will be neither the original-in-English only, nor the author-helped-by-original only, but a product rather than a sum of the two.(7)

Two particular aspects of Egan's considerable achievement should be noted. First, register of language. Egan sticks at all times toan emphatic modern register that avoids both archaismandneologism,andis therefore a pleasure to read. Second, the choral odes. Here Egan scores a remarkable success by keeping in these notoriously tricky passages (very difficult in Greek, never mind in English) to this register and rigorously avoiding any lapse into translatorese of the type parodied by Ezra Pound in his *Homage to Sextus Propertius*,

> Oh couch made happy by my long delectations.

Egan's *Medea* is, then, one of the great translations of this era and gives the lie to Virginia Woolf's suggestion that reading Greek in translation is a waste of time because translators only offer a vague equivalent.

As Egan himself has said, poetry

> Consists of that essence which can be translated. (8)

And here *is*.

NOTES ON THE TEXT

The text of Medea followed here is that of D. L. Page, Euripides - Medea, Edited with Introduction and Commentary (Oxford 1978). The traditional numbering of the lines has been retained, although a few spurious lines have been omitted.

NOTES

1. W. B. Yeats, *Explorations* (London 1962), page 439.

2. Desmond Egan, Third Margaret Heavey Memorial Lecture, delivered at University College, Galway, March 11, 1988. (Published in *The Death of Metaphor*, Selected Prose).

3. Cf. W. Arrowsmith in *Euripides*, ed. E. Segal (Englewood Cliffs, N.J. 1968), 13-33.

4. K. Marx, *Grundrisse*, trans. M. Nicolaus (Harmondsworth 1973), Introduction, page 111.

5. M. B. Arthur, *Yale Review* 71 (1982), page 539.

6. For *Medea* see D. L. Page, *Euripides , Medea* (Oxford 1978; c.f. above) and the following articles: E. Schlesinger in Segal (note 3), 70-89; M. Shaw, *Classical Philology* 70 (1975), 255-66; P. E. Easterling, *Yale Classical Studies* 25 (1977), 1977-91; B. Knox, *ibid.*, 193-225; B. Arkins, *Ramus* 11 (1982), 116-23.

7. R. Lattimore in *On Translation*, ed. R. A. Brower (New York 1966), 49. Lattimore translated, *inter alia*, the *Iliad* and *Odyssey* of Homer, the first hailed by W. Arrowsmith as 'The finest translation of Homer ever made into the English language'; the second by G. Highet as 'the best *Odyssey* in modern English'.

8. Desmond Egan, *Studies* 76 (1987), page 227.

DRAMATIS PERSONAE

Nurse

Tutor

Medea

Chorus of Corinthian Ladies

Creon, King of Corinth

Jason

Aegeus, King of Athens

Messenger

Two Children of Medea

Scene: before Jason's house at Corinth

EURIPIDES: MEDEA
Translated by Desmond Egan

Nurse:
How I wish that the Argo had never skimmed through
the blue Symplegades to the land of Colchis,
and that the felled pine had never toppled
in Glen Pelion to put oars into
the hands of heroes; and that they had never
gone after the Golden Fleece for Pelias
- because then my lady, Medea,
would not have set sail to the towers of Iolcos
lovesick for Jason;
nor would she, having persuaded Pelias' daughters
to murder their father, now live here in Corinth with   10
her man and her children, only gladdening those
to whose land she arrived in her exile
when she was completely at Jason's service
(and indeed that's the best security
when a wife is not at loggerheads with her husband.)
Now all is hatred! Even those closest to him are disgusted
because Jason has betrayed both his children and my Lady
by taking a royal bride to bed -
marrying the daughter of Creon, the King.
In her humiliation, poor Medea   20
shouts curses, screams about the great pledge by the right hand,
calls on the Gods to witness
what kind of thanks she is getting from Jason.
She lies indoors without food, yielding to her misery
wasting away with crying all the time.
Now that she realises she's been discarded by her husband,
she won't even look up, won't raise her face from the ground.
She pays no more attention to friends who try to give her advice
thanshe would to a stone or to a wave of the sea.

But sometimes she turns her white neck   30
and weeps to herself for her dear father,
for her own country and her home: for all that she
betrayed in coming here
with the man who has now disgraced her.
Only through disaster has the unfortunate woman learned
what a great thing it is not to lose your own country.
She has turned against her children, gets no joy out of seeing them -
and I'm afraid she may decide on some other plan of action.
She's a dangerous woman: anyone who becomes her enemy
won't get away lightly!

But here are her boys - they've finished running   40
and here they come, mindless of their mother's sufferings because
no young mind likes to be depressed for long.
Tutor:
Ancient servant of my Lady's palace! What are you doing
standing at the gates here alone
whimpering to yourself over your misfortune?
How is it that Medea wants you to leave her on her own?
Nurse:
Look, old man, teacher of Jason's children -
surely the sufferings and misfortunes of our masters
touch the heart of us servants as well?   50
I have fallen into such a state of depression
that I just *had* to make my way here
to cry out to heaven and earth about Medea's situation.
Tutor:
Has the unfortunate woman not stopped weeping yet?
Nurse:
I'm amazed at you! Her misery is only beginning - it's not even
  half over
Tutor:
She's foolish - if I may say so about my master -
she doesn't even know of the latest misfortune.
Nurse:
What is it, old man? Come on, don't hold back on me!
Tutor:
Nothing. I take back what I said.

Nurse:

Please, I beg you, don't hide it from your fellow-servant.   60
I'll keep my mouth shut if that's the way you want it.

Tutor:

Though I didn't pretent to, I heard someone saying,
as I approached the gaming place where old folk
sit around the holy fountain of Peirene,
that Creon, King of this land, has made up his mind   70
to drive out the children along with their mother
from Corinthian soil. But now, whether this is true or not
I cannot say. I hope it's not.

Nurse:

Will Jason tolerate such treatment of his children
even though he has fallen-out with their mother?

Tutor:

Old ties are abandoned for new ones
and that man is not well-disposed to this house.

Nurse:

We're ruined if we add fresh trouble
to old, before we see an end to the first.

Tutor:

Yes - but this is not a good time for her to find out   80
so keep quiet and don't say a word!

Nurse:

Children, do you hear what kind of father you have?
Damn him! But no - he's still my master
even if he's now shown-up as disloyal to those near to him.

Tutor:

And what human being is not? Did you only learn lately
that everyone loves himself more than his neighbour?
Rightly so, for some! - but others act out of greed:
their father, for example, loves these children less than his bed!

Nurse:

Go on into the palace, children. Things will work out.
For your part, try as best you can to keep them on their own   90
and don't approach their mother - she's beside herself. Already
I have seen her glaring at them like a bull
as if to do them harm. There will be no end
to her rage - as I well know! - until she works it off on someone.
I only hope it's on her enemies and not on her friends.

Medea:
  Aaah!
  What an unfortunate creature I am! What misery I endure!
  No, no! I wish I were dead.
Nurse:
  Dear children, this is what I was saying: your mother
  is heartbroken, she's not herself.
  Better go quickly to the palace   100
  and don't come within sight of her.
  Don't go next or near the woman! Be careful of
  that wild streak in her, her hateful side,
  her ruthlessness.
  (*Medea screams*)
  Off with you! Go inside as quickly as you can.
  It's obvious that a cloud of misery has appeared
  and will soon be flashing with lightning, with an even worse rage.
  What will she do then,
  passionate and reckless woman that she is,
  when her mind is eaten-into by these wrongs?   110
  (*The Tutor brings the children into the house*)
Medea:
  Aaaaah!
  Unfortunate wretch that I am, I have suffered, ah, ah, have I suffered
  to talk about! Ah you are ruined,
  children of a hated mother! May you be destroyed
  with your father! May the whole line disappear!
Nurse:
  No no no! Ah me, poor unfortunate woman -
  why should your children be blamed for
  their father's crime? Why should you hate them?
  Oh little ones I hope you don't suffer what I am so afraid of.
  Those who have power have also horrible tempers -
  rarely under control, they mostly give orders   120
  and don't too easily get over their anger.
  It's better to deal only with one's equals.
  For my part, may I grow old in security
  if I may not do so in greatness.
  A word about moderation: in brief
  the name says everything. Human beings are far better off
  if they practise it. Excess

is no help to man.
When a God becomes enraged he doles out
greater destruction on a house.   130
(*Enter Chorus of Corinthian women*)
Chorus:
I have heard the voice, heard the cry
of this unfortunate woman from Colchis.
It is still in the air. Speak old woman!
From the doorway I have heard her wailing in the hall.
Nurse I take no pleasure at all in the misfortunes of this home
since I decided to take sides with it.
Nurse:
There is no home! Already that is over.
My master now shares the bed of a princess;   140
my mistress is wasting away indoors.
Not one of her friends
can comfort her in any way with the voice of reason.
Medea:
Aaaah ...!
I wish a bolt of lightning from heaven would strike
right through my head! What have I to live-for anymore?
No, no. I wish I could find release in death
and leave this hateful life once and for all.
Chorus:
Zeus, and earth and light! do you hear
the cry which this unfortunate young wife
so mournfully raises?   150
For what reason, rash woman, have you a wish
for that awful resting place?
Would you speed-up death, the end of everything?
No, do not pray for that.
Even if your husband
worships a new mistress
do not be so distressed over it.
Zeus will see that you have justice. Do not pine away
with grief for the one whose bed you shared.
Medea:
Great Justice, Themis, and Lady Artemis   160
just see what I am suffering! I who bound him over -
that accursed husband - with solemn oaths.

May I yet see him and his new bride
  - they, the two of them who dared to do me wrong -
  destroyed with their palace and everything!
  O my father! O city of Colchis! I have lost you both
  because I dishonourably murdered my brother.

Nurse:

  Do you hear what she says? She calls on
  Themis, Goddess of vows, and on Zeus
  guardian of oaths among mortals.   170
  There is no chance that my mistress will give-up her fury
   for any small revenge.

Chorus:

  If only she would come out into the open,
  accept the implications
  of what has been said
  she might get rid of this rage that weighs her down
  and of her mind's obsession.
  Now may my own good will
  towards my friends not desert me!
  Go and bring her here   180
  from the house; tell her I am well-disposed.
  Hurry, before she does something awful to those within
  because her grief is driving her in that direction.

Nurse:

  I'll do it but I doubt
  that you can persuade my Lady.
  Still, I'll take the trouble, to please you,
  though she glares - with the look of a lioness who has just whelped -
  at her servant when any of us
  comes near her with a message.
  You would not be wrong to describe   190
  those men of old as uncouth and ignorant, who composed
  songs for feasts and festivals and banquets -
  the sweet music of life! -
  because none of them ever discovered a way
  in their music and many-toned song
  to get rid of man's abominable suffering, out of which death
  and misfortune bring houses to ruin.
  And yet it would be great if human beings
  were healed with songs. When a feast is lavish   200

why should people sing loudly to no effect?
No doubt, the moment has enjoyment enough in itself
- the fullness of the feast - to suffice...
Chorus:
  I have heard her cry out with grief,
  piercingly she laments her misfortune -
  a faithless husband, traitor to her bed.
  Having suffered injustice, she calls on the Gods
  - on Themis, Zeus' binder of oaths
  who once led her across to Greece   210
  on the opposite side,
  through the night wave though the straits
  through the salty and limitless sea.
  (Enter Medea)
Medea:
  Corinthian women, I have come outside
  in case you might somehow blame *me.* I know of many
  who are called arrogant: some from keeping to themselves;
  others from travelling about; still others, who lead a quiet life,
  and end up with a reputation for laziness.
  Justice does not lie in the judgment of man -
  before discerning a person's character clearly
  a man can hate at sight though he has suffered no wrong.
  A stranger most of all must conform to city ways
  (yet I don't admire the citizen who, out of prejudice,
  is bitter about neighbours through ignorance).
  This unexpected disaster that struck me
  has broken my spirit. I'm devastated.
  I have lost the joy of living, friends, I want only to die.
  In that man I could find all that was beautiful
  - my husband, now turned into the worst of men.
  Of all that has life and intelligence
  we women are the most unfortunate ones - we   230
  who first of all buy - like the highest bidder! - a husband
  and end-up with a master over our body.
  But having no man is worse misfortune
  and here lies the greatest risk:
  is he good or useless? Divorce
  does not help a woman; one must not reject one's husband!
  Now a woman who faces new customs and usages

being untutored, would really need inspiration
to know how best she should deal with her bedmate.
If, however, we pass this hard test   240
and the husband live in harmony, not yoked against his will
then life is enviable. Otherwise, we ought to die.
A man who gets fed-up from being in the house
can go out, relieve his boredom
whereas we women must look to him alone.
Of course *they* say we live a life free of danger
at home while they go to battle with the spear ...
They're making a mistake: three times would I prefer to take arms
than give birth once!   250
And it's not even the same story for me as for you.
You have a city, a father's home,
a life of fulfillment, the company of friends ...
I am on my own, a stateless person, humiliated by my husband,
snatched from a foreign country
and no mother, no brother, no relation
to comfort me in my distress.
So, I would ask only this much of you:
if I find any way, any chance
of paying back my husband for these wrongs say nothing!   260
A woman may in other matters be full of fear
and cowardly at the sight of battle or of the sword
but when she happens to be wronged in bed
no mind is more bloodthirsty!

Chorus:
I will do that. Justly will you pay back your husband,
Medea. I don't wonder at your grieving over misfortunes.
(Enter Creon)
But I see Creon, King of this land
coming, the bearer of new decrees.

Creon: 270
I have commanded that you with the bitter look, the husband-hater,
you, Medea, should get out of this country
into exile, taking with you your two offspring.
Do not delay at all! I am here to enforce this decree
and will not return to my palace
until I have you outside the borders of this country.

Medea:

No! No! I'm finished, this is the end!
My enemies are in full sail
and I have no safe landing from destruction!
But let me ask you, wronged and all as I am,
why, Creon, do you banish me from here? 280

Creon:

I am afraid of you. No need to beat about the bush
- afraid you might do permanent harm to my daughter.
I have several reasons for this fear.
You are by nature cunning, skilled in evil arts
and furious at losing your man's bed.
You have threatened - so they tell me - to do something to
father, bride and bridegroom
so I will take action to prevent that happening.
Better for us to be hated by you, woman, now,
than to relent and regret it afterwards. 290

Medea:

Unfair, unfair!
This is not the first time, but one of many, Creon
that my reputation has hurt me, and done me real harm.
A father with judgment should never, ever,
have his children well educated -
apart from the useless knowledge they acquire,
they only earn the dislike and envy of neighbours.
Give new ideas to the ignorant
and you will seem foolish rather than wise.
If you are considered cleverer than those who have the reputation
you will only be odious in people's eyes. 300
I myself share-in this fate -
because I'm clever, some envy me;
to others I seem difficult and I'm not even *very* clever!
You dread me also in case you suffer something unpleasant?
That's not my way Creon, do not be afraid
that I would commit a crime against a king.
So why are you wronging me? You gave your daughter
to the one your heart desired. True, I hate my husband -
still I admit that *you* acted reasonably 310
and don't begrudge you that things have worked-out.
Let the marriage go ahead and good luck to you - but let me

live-on in this country because, even though wronged,
I will behave myself, made docile by those in power.
Creon:
You speak words soothing to hear but in your heart
I am afraid you plan to do evil
and I trust you even less than before
because a quick-tempered woman - or man, for that matter -
is easier to guard-against than a clever, silent one.
So , go without delay. Say no more!   320
This is final. No scheming of yours will make it possible
that you stay among us, an enemy of mine.
Medea:
No - I beg you, no! in the name of your newly-married daughter!
Creon:
You're wasting your words. You would never persuade me.
Medea:
Will you really drive me out and not hear my request?
Creon:
I don't like you better than my own family.
Medea:
Oh native land! how much I remember you now.
Creon:
Apart from my children, I love my city most.
Medea:
Unfortunate me! What a curse on mortals is love.
Creon:
I think that depends on how things work out.   330
Medea:
Zeus! never forget the one responsible for all this!
Creon:
Move, foolish woman and rid us of our problem.
Medea:
I have enough trouble. I don't need any more!
Creon:
Move! You'll be expelled by force, at the hands of my servants.
Medea:
Don't do it, Creon! I beg you!
Creon:
It seems that you wish to make trouble, woman!

Medea:

No, I'll go! That's not what I want from you.

Creon:

Then why do you force me? Why haven't you left the country?

Medea:

Let me wait this one day, just,
and give thought to how I'll go   340
and find some base for my children - since their father
never bothers about providing for his offspring.
Pity them! - you too are the father of children
and it is natural that you should have sympathy.
I don't worry about myself if we go into exile
but feel sad that *they* should suffer as well.

Creon:

I am not at all ruthless at heart
and have suffered plenty in the past simply through relenting ...
This time also, woman, I think I'm making a mistake -
still, Medea, you shall have what you ask. But I warn you   350
if tomorrow the light of the Sun-god look on you
and your sons within the boundaries of this country,
you shall die! This sentence is irrevocable.
Now: if you need to stay, stay for one day only -
so that you cannot do any of the terrible things I fear.
(Exit Creon)

Chorus:

Unfortunate woman
wretched, wretched in you sufferings!
Where will you turn? What protection can you find,
or house or country as salvation
from disaster?   360
Zeus has driven you, Medea,
into an inexorable wave of evil!

Medea:

I have fared badly on every side, who can deny it?
But that's not the case just now, don't you think it!
Some troubles lie in store for the newlyweds
and no little trouble for those who brought them together!
Do you really think I would have played-up to that fellow
unless for a reason; to plot something? No!
Otherwise I would never have spoken to him or clung to his hands.

He has reached such heights of foolishness   370
that, even though he could spoil my plans
by throwing me out of the country, he has allowed me
to remain for one day - a day in which I'll make corpses of
my three enemies: father, daughter and husband.
I have so many ways of getting rid of them
that I'm not sure, my friends, which to try first -
whether I'll set the bridal house on fire
or, having gone through the palace silently to their bed
drive a sharp sword through their guts.
Only one consideration holds me back: if I'm caught   380
going into the palace with such a scheme in mind
I shall be killed and give my enemies something to laugh at.
(Pause)
Best do it the obvious way - the one where I am by nature
most skilled: finish them off by poison!
Yes, that's the way.
And so they're dead: what city now will allow me entry?
What friend abroad grant asylum, a place of refuge,
and save my life?
No one. I'll delay here a short while
and, in case any tower of safety appears,   390
carry out this murder cunningly, on the quiet ...
If bad luck is about to drive me away frustrated
I'll grab a sword myself - even if I die for it -
and kill them. I'm prepared to risk anything.
No! by Hecate - by that goddess whom I honour most,
whom I have chosen as my collaborator
and who has a place in the sanctuary of my home - by Hecate
none of these people will break my heart and get away with it!
I'll give them a bitter, yes a painful marriage,
my banishment for a sad affinity!
Come on Medea, overlook nothing you know -   400
Medea; The Plotter! - about plotting and scheming.
Make a start to this deed of horror. Here's the test of your courage.
Look what you are enduring! You must not become a laughing stock
through this Sisyphus-like marriage of Jason
-you from the line of a noble father and of the Sun-god.
You know better. And don't forget : you're a woman -
useless to do anything of real value, hah

- but very clever at hatching every kind of harm!
Chorus:
  Uphill they flow, the waters of the sacred rivers   410
  and order and everything turns upside-down;
  treachery in men; no oath sworn on the gods
  has power to last ...
  Legends about us women, however,
  will change our status and bring us glory.
  Yes, honour is coming to the female race -
  no longer will we have a low standing.   420

  Muses of the ancients, give up your song!
  Your singing is only about our faithlessness
  - for Phoebus, Lord of music,
  did not grant inspiration through the lyre
  to our female mentality
  otherwise I would have sung a melody in counterpoint
  to that of the males! The centuries have as much
  to tell about *our* life as about man's.   430

You, Medea, sailed off from your father's palace
  with maddened heart you cut between the two clashing
  rocks of the sea. You are living
  in a foreign land yet have lost your marriage bed
  for a husbandless couch -
  unfortunate woman! Now exile
  will drive you from these parts, dishonoured.
  Gone is the force of oaths. No shame remains
  in the length and breadth of Greece: it has flown into the sky.   440

For you, pitiable woman,
  no father's house as a haven to rest-in
  away from your troubles; and another princess
  whose bed has more appeal than yours
  is set to rule in your house.
  (Enter Jason)
Jason:
  This is not the first time but one of many that I have noticed
  a bad temper is impossible to deal-with!
  You could have remained in this country and kept your home,

if you had accepted gracefully the plans of your rulers -
'but for your reckless comments you will now be expelled
          from the land.   450
It doesn't matter to *me:* don't for a second stop
telling people that Jason is the worst of men!
  - but for what you have said against those in authority
consider yourself very lucky to have been punished only by exile.
For my part, I have continually tried to calm the anger
of the infuriated King. I wanted you to stay
but you would not give up your foolishness - all the time
abusing the royal family. So you will be thrown out of the place.
In spite of that, not wanting to renounce my friends,
I have come here to give thought to your future, woman,   460
so that you may not go destitute into exile with the children
or be in need of anything. Banishment, you know, brings with it
many hardships. Even if you hate me
I could never think badly of you.
Medea:
O worst of the very worst! - the greatest insult
I can put into words for your rotten cowardice -
you came to me! Yes, you came, you whom I now hate the most!
but not from courage, or daring did you come
to show your face to those friends you wronged
  - no, but from the worst of all human failings,   470
shamelessness! Still, it's good that you have come
because it will relieve my feelings
to give you abuse - and you won't enjoy listening.
I'll begin at the very beginning.
I saved your skin (as those Greeks know
who sailed with you on the *Argo*)
when you were sent to yoke-up the fire-breathing bulls
and sow the deadly field with dragon's teeth.
I also killed the serpent who coiled round the Golden Fleece   480
never sleeping, guarding it with his twisted coils,
and raised for you the light of deliverance.
Then I betrayed my own father and my home
and went off with you to Iolcos under Mount Pelion,
a woman more eager than wise.
I killed Pelias in the most painful of ways -
at the hands of his own children. I finished the whole house.

And having got all this out of me, lowest of the low!
you betrayed me, found yourself a new bed
after our children were born . If you were still childless   490
your lusting for another bed might have been forgivable!
But no! Respect for our oath is forgotten. I wonder
do you imagine the ancient Gods no longer have power
and that new laws apply to humans nowadays?
- because I know you are a perjurer in my regard.
Poor right hand which often you took hold of
and these knees - how vainly were they clung-to by an evil man!
I was disappointed in all my hopes.
Look, I'll ask you something as if we were friends
- as if I could hope for fair play from you! -   500
nevertheless - and this question will show you up even more -
where do I turn now? Back to my father's house
which I betrayed for you along with my country, to come here?
Back to the unfortunate daughters of Pelias? They would surely
receive me well since I killed their father!
Here is how things stand: to my friends at home
I have become an enemy; those whom I should not have harmed
have turned hostile because I helped you.
Yes, you made me some object of envy
among the women of Greece, in return for it all!   510
A wonderful, faithful husband! How unfortunate I am -
so I flee having been thrown out of the country
without friends, on my own, with my abandoned children!
Some reputation for a newly-wed husband - that
your children andthe woman who saved you wander round as beggars!
Great Zeus! why, why have you given mortals clear means of detecting
counterfeit gold - but where man is concerned,
where it is really necessary to distinguish the bad,
you have stamped no clear mark on the body?

Chorus:
That anger is terrible, it is incurable   520
when friendship turns to hatred.

Jason:
It seems that I must not lack eloquence
if, like the alert helmsman of a ship,
I am to escape with a narrow strip of sail
from your continuous, loudmouthed, abuse, woman!

Well - since you make so much of what you have done -
I hold that Aphrodite alone of Gods and of men
was the saviour of my voyage!
You have a clever mind, no doubt - but it would be pointless
to describe how it came about that Eros compelled you   530
with his sure arrows to save my life!
I won't labour the point in detail,
and whenever you did help me it was not bad
- though as regards my welfare
you got more than you gave - and I can prove it.
For a start, you live in Greece and not in a barbarian land,
so you know what justice is -
the rule of law - rather than some ruler's whim.
All Greeks have come to know about your cleverness;
you're famous. If you had lived at the ends of the earth   540
you would never have been heard of.
For my part, I want neither gold in my palace
nor to sing a sweeter song than Orpheus
if my name does not become renowned.
So far, I have spoken about *my* adventures
but you were the one who started this argument.
As for your attacks on my royal marriage -
in this matter I will show that I was first of all wise
then prudent and lastly a real friend to you
and to my children. No - keep your peace!   550
When I came here to Corinth from Iolchos,
dragging many terrible worries with me,
what better solution could I have found
than to marry the King's daughter? I, a mere exile!
It's not - what is tormenting you - that I hated your bed,
stricken with desire for a different partner, no
nor out of any ambition to produce numerous children
- those born already are enough, I find no fault in them -
it was most of all that we might live well
and not want for anything. I realised that   560
a poor man's friends all avoid him.
I wanted to rear the children in a fitting way
and have brothers for those children of yours.
I would have made one of you all and, uniting as a family,
we would have lived happily. What need have you of more children?

but it would be an advantage to me to help the existing ones
through those yet to be born. Did I plan things badly?
You would not have said so only that sex annoys you!
Anyhow it has come to this: women imagine
that if all's well in bed, they have everything,   570
but as soon as something goes wrong sexually
they see the best, the finest relationship as the biggest battlefield.
Better for mortals that children were bred some other way
and that the female race did not exist!
If that were so, no curse would have befallen man!

Chorus:

Jason, you have made a good defence
nevertheless you seem to me - even if I speak indiscreetly -
to have acted unjustly in betraying your wife.

Medea:

Indeed I *am* totally different from most mortals.
For me, whoever is clever at arguing when in the wrong   580
deserves the greatest punishment - for this reason, that
having the nerve to dress-up injustice cleverly with his tongue,
he grows reckless with hypocrisy. But really, he's not that clever!
So you needn't make any pretences in my regard
and talk plausibly - one argument will flatten you:
you could, if you weren't so low, have gone ahead with this marriage
after persuading me - and not in secrecy from those close to you.

Jason:

Oh I'm sure you would have accepted my plan
if I had mentioned this marriage to you in advance! You who even
still make no effort to get rid of your bitterness.   590

Medea:

This is not what stopped you from telling me - it's that a foreign wife
would not have helped your standing as you grew older!

Jason:

Take good note of this:
it was not for the sake of a woman
that I married the royal bride whom I now have
but as I've already explained - because I wished to save
you and breed royal brothers
for my children: *to safeguard my house, to make it secure.*

Medea:

May I have no prosperous but rather an unhappy life

in preference to your 'security' that would torment my mind!   600
Jason:

Can't you learn to change that prayer and show more sense?
Don't let what is to your benefit ever seem a drawback
nor your good fortune appear the opposite!
Medea:

Go on, insult me! You with your safe place of refuge,
while I, abandoned, will be in exile from here.
Jason:

You chose that - blame nobody else!
Medea:

What did I do? Did I marry again and betray you?
Jason:

No - but you called down wicked curses on kings!
Medea:

And on your house *I* happen to be the curse!
Jason:

Look, I don't intend to argue with you further about all this
but if you want any help from me   610
(either for the children or for your own life in exile)
just say so - I'm prepared to give with a generous hand
and send introductions to my friends abroad who will look-after you.
If you don't want these things, woman, you're a fool!
Give up your rage and you will fare much better.
Medea:

I would not make use of any friends of yours
nor accept a thing from you. Don't give us anything!
The gifts of an evil man bring no luck with them.
Jason:

Very well. Therefore I call on the Gods to witness
that I am willing to help you and the children in every way   620
but you do not like what is good for you and out of stubbornness
push your friends to one side. As a result, you'll suffer all the more.
Medea:

Off with you! You're overcome with desire for
your new conquest, after spending so long away from her bedroom!
Well, be married - but maybe, with the help of Zeus,
you will marry such a marriage as you will yet regret!
(Exit Jason and attendants)

Chorus:
Uncontrolled love
does not bring honour
or goodness to men
- but if Aphrodite come in moderation   630
no other God is so gracious.
Never, O Goddess, shoot
from your golden bow at me
the inescapable arrow dipped in desire.

May temperance protect me -
most beautiful gift of the gods
and may terrible Aphrodite never ever
drive me mad for another bed
nor visit upon me any troublesome rages,
any of those endless rows   640
- but having respect for peaceful union
may she be a keen judge in women's affairs.
O land of my fathers, O home
may I never, never, end-up stateless,
living a life of desperation.
An intolerable existence! pitiable
and full of suffering.
By death, by death may I first be overcome
before encountering such a day
- because no pain is worse   650
than that of losing one's fatherland.

We have all seen this: we do not need
to hear anyone else's story.
Neither city nor friend
showed you pity as you endured
the worst suffering of all.
Let him perish miserably, that man who is accustomed
not to honour his friends by revealing   660
the sincere key to his thoughts! For my part,
may I never have such a friend.
(*Enter Aegeus and retainers*)
Aegeus:
Greetings, Medea. No one knows

a sweeter start than this to conversation with a friend.
Medea:
  And greetings to you Aegeus, son of wise Pandion!
  Where have you been, that you visit this country?
Aegeus:
  I have just left the ancient oracle of Phoebus.
Medea:
  Why did you go as far as the centre of prophecy, Delphi?
Aegeus:
  Trying to find out how I might have children.
Medea:
  By the Gods - have you lived childless for this long, ?   670
Aegeus:
  Yes, I'm childless through some mischance of fate.
Medea:
  Have you a wife or are you unmarried?
Aegeus:
  O, I am not without experience of the marriage-bed.
Medea:
  And what did Phoebus say to you about children?
Aegeus:
  Words too deep for man to understand.
Medea:
  Is it right to let me know the oracle of the God?
Aegeus:
  Of course - since it calls for a subtle mind.
Medea:
  What did it say? Tell me, if it's proper to hear it.
Aegeus:
  Do not open the wineskin's foot.
Medea:
  Until you do what, or go to what country?   680
Aegeus:
  Until I go back to the home of my ancestors.
Medea:
  Then why did you have to sail to this land?
Aegeus:
  There's a certain Pittheus, King of Troezen -
Medea:
  - The son of Pelops, they say; a very pious man.

Aegeus:
I wish to consult him about the God's oracle.
Medea:
A wise man indeed - and knowledgeable in such matters.
Aegeus:
To me he's also the friendliest of allies.
Medea:
Well I hope you're fortunate and get what you want.
Aegeus:
But why do you look so dejected, so wasted in appearance?
Medea:
O, Aegeus, my husband is of all men the very worst.   690
Aegeus:
What do you mean? Tell me why you are depressed.
Medea:
Jason is doing me wrong though I never treated him badly.
Aegeus:
What did he do on you? Tell me more plainly.
Medea:
He has taken another woman as mistress.
Aegeus:
Surely he never dared to do that most shameful thing?
Medea:
Be certain sure he did! Once his beloved, I am now discarded.
Aegeus:
Did he fall in love or just get tired of your bed?
Medea:
O deeply in love! But not faithful to his friends.
Aegeus:
Well away with him if he's *that* bad!
Medea:
He desperately wanted to be related to a king.   700
Aegeus:
Which king is giving his daughter to him? Tell me the rest ...
Medea:
It's Creon who rules over this Corinthian territory.
Aegeus:
Lady, it's understandable that you should be downhearted.
Medea:
This is the end. And I'm being driven-out as well.

Aegeus:

By whom? You're talking about another injustice, now!

Medea:

Creon is driving me into exile from Corinth.

Aegeus:

Does Jason allow it? I don't give him much praise.

Medea:

In *word* he doesn't
-but he's prepared to put up with it!
Now I beg you by your very beard -   710
at your knees I beg you -
pity oh pity me in my misfortune
don't just look-on as I'm got rid of, abandoned
- take me into your country, into your palace
and, by the Gods, may your love bear fruit
in children, may you yourself die happy.
You don't realise that you have made a discovery -
because I will end your childlessness, I'll enable you
to sow the seeds of children: I know such medicines!

Aegeus:

For several reasons, Lady, I'm anxious
to do you this favour. Firstly for the sake of the Gods;   720
and secondly, for the birth of those children you promise -
because I'm at a complete loss in this regard.
This much I promise you, Medea, if you come to my land
I will try to be an honourable ally of yours -
but, Lady, I tell you right now, in advance,
I shall not connive-at bringing you out of this country .
However, if you can make your own way to where I live
you shall remain there unharmed. I will not turn you over to anyone.
From here, though, you will have to go on your own
because I must be above reproach with my hosts.   730

Medea:

Agreed. Now, if I could have a pledge for this
I would have been treated well by you in every single way.

Aegeus:

Do you not trust me? What's your problem?

Medea:

I do trust you - but the house of Pelias is hostile to me
and so is Creon. Bound by an oath, you would never

hand me over if they wanted to take me away.
Having made a promise without swearing it
you might take their side and give-in, in no time,
to their demands. My position is vulnerable
whereas they have wealth and a royal house on their side. 740
Aegeus:
You have shown real foresight in you words
so if that's what seems best to you, I shall not refuse.
Indeed it will be safest for me, also,
to have an excuse to give your enemies
and it suits your situation even more. So: name the Gods!
Medea:
Swear by the plain of Earth, by my father's father
Helios the Sun, and add-in all the race of the Gods.
Aegeus:
What do you want me to do or not-do? Say it.
Medea:
Never to expel me from your land, yourself,
nor while you're alive, to hand me over, willingly, 750
to any of my enemies who wishes to take me away!
Aegeus:
I swear by Earth, by the pure majesty of the Sun
and by all the Gods, to stand by what I hear you proposing.
Medea:
That will do - but what should you suffer for breaking this oath?
Aegeus:
Whatever happens to impious men.
Medea:
Go and fare you well! All this is fine.
I will arrive at your city as quickly as possible,
having done what I intend and having got what I want.
Chorus:
May Hermes, son of Maia, Lord of Journeys
lead you home; and this thing which you desire - 760
may it soon be yours, because
Aegeus, you seem to me
an honourable man.
Medea:
O Zeus! and Justice, daughter of Zeus! O Light of the Sun!
- now, friends, shall we overwhelm my enemies.

We are on course.
Now there's hope for vengence on my foes.
This man, in the very area where I was most under pressure,
has emerged to harbour my plans:
from him will I fasten my ship's cable   770
when I reach the fortess and city of Pallas Athene.
Now shall I tell you all I have in mind
- only don't expect my words to be enjoyable.
I'll send one of my servants to Jason
asking him come and see me.
When he arrives I'll speak soothing words -
say I agree with him; that all is well
and that the royal marriage by which he betrayed me
is well planned, all for the best.
I will ask that my children remain here -   780
not that I would ever abandon them in a hostile country,
my children for my enemies to insult! no-
but in order to kill the King's daughter by this trick.
I'll send them carrying in their hands presents for the bride -
a fine robe and a golden wreath.
If she accepts and puts-on my dress
she will die horribly, as will anyone who touches the girl -
- such will be the poison I smear my presents with.
But, enough of that for now.   790
I cry with grief at what I still have to do.
Because I will kill the children,yes
my own children. No one will take them from me.
When I've made havoc of the House of Jason
then I shall leave the country and get away from the slaughter of
my dearest ones, after I dare carry-out that most impious of acts.
It's intolerable, friends, to be mocked-at by one's enemies.
So let this be! What good is life to me? No fatherland,
no home, no escape from my miseries ...
I made a mistake once, when I gave up   800
my father's house, taken-in by the talk of a Greek -
a Greek who, with the help of the Gods, will now pay the price.
He shall never again lay eyes on those sons of mine alive, no,
nor have children by his new bride
- since the bitch must die
and horribly, by my poison.

Let no one think me spineless or weak or tame!
- the reverse, in fact is the case -
I'm relentless to my enemies, gentle only to friends:
the life of such a one is the most glorious of all.   810
Chorus:
You have told me your plan
so I wish to help you - and since I support human law
I say, do not do it!
Medea:
There is no other way - but I forgive you for saying that
because you have never gone through the suffering that I have.
Chorus:
But will you dare, woman, to kill your own two sons?
Medea:
I will - because that's how my husband can be tormented the most!
Chorus:
You would become the most miserable of all women.
Medea:
So what! All arguments for restraint are useless.
(Enter Nurse)
There you are! Go and bring me Jason   820
- you're the one I call - on in all matters of trust.
Tell no one anything of my intentions
support me in this and you'll prove yourself a *woman!*
Chorus:
Happy the Athenians, sons of Erechtheus, of old !
born of the blessed Gods, in a sacred, unconquered land,
taking their nourishment from
supreme Wisdom always moving gracefully
through the luminous air. There, once upon a time, it is said   830
the Nine Pierian Muses, the pure ones
gave birth to golden Harmony.

A people sprung, too, from the waters of the smooth-flowing
Cephisus, where they say that Aphrodite of Cyprus drew water
breathing gentle breaths of wind on the land;
where too, those Loves, companions of Wisdom
and co-workers in all kinds of goodness,
escort Aphrodite, constantly strewing on her hair   840

perfumed garlands of rose.

How then could this city of sacred rivers,
this land that provides
safe escort for friends, receive you,
murderess of her children,
an impious woman, among her other citizens?   850
Think of the shock to your own offspring.
Think about murder and all it destroys ...
Do not, on our knees we implore you
by everything, by everyone -
do not kill your children!

Where will you find the toughness, either of mind
or of heart and hand
to kill your own
carrying-out this terrible decision?
When you look at your children   860
how can you keep yourself from weeping
at their murderous fate? When your sons kneel begging
you will never be able
to stain, with relentless mind,
your hand with their blood.
(Enter Jason)

Jason:
I come at your bidding: although you are hostile
you shall not be denied this much. I will listen to
whatever new request you wish to make, woman.

Medea:
Jason, for what I said, I ask you
forgive me - maybe there is a chance that you   870
would put up with my fits of temper
because of the love there has been between us.
I've thought about your arguments and
now I'm disgusted with myself. Reckless fool, am I mad?
Do I bear ill will to those who only wish me well?
Why have I fallen out with the rulers of this land
and with a husband who is doing his best by us:
a royal marriage and the creation of brothers
for my sons? Will I not put aside my annoyance?

What complaint have I when the Gods look after me well?
Haven't I got children? Do I not know that we're in exile here   880
from my own country, without friends ...?
Realising all this I saw I was being most unwise,
in a rage without good reason.
So I must give you credit. Now *you* seem wise to me
in developing this relationship for us. *I'm* the stupid one
who ought to have shared-in these plans;
to have co-operated; to have stood by your marriage
and be happy to wait-on your bride!
But we women are what we are - I won't say, evil -
so you should not imitate my failing   890
and match foolishness with foolishness.
I apologise. I admit I got things wrong.
Now I've arrived at a better understanding of everything.
O children, children come here! Come out of the house
and greet him. Say goodbye to him
with me. Give up your recent bad feeling
(*Enter Children*)
towards friends, along with your mother!
- because we have made peace, we have put away anger.
Take his right hand. Yet how sad it all is!   900
How I'm haunted by the unknown future!
Will you, children, for as long as you live
stretch out to me a loving arm in this way? Ah me,
how easily *I* cry! How full of fear!
This quarrel with your father, ended at last,
Ii has filled these soft eyes with tears.
Chorus:
And from my eyes too has the pale tear started.
O may the course of evil advance no further!
Jason:
I praise you in this, woman, and do not blame you for the rest.
It is natural that any female should get annoyed
with a husband who manages to arrange another marriage!   910
But your heart has had a turn for the better. Although it's taken time,
you have opted for the wiser course
and that is the act of a clever woman.
As for you, children: your father has not forgotten you
but with the help of the Gods has provided real security for you.

I believe that you will take your place yet along with your brothers -
at the top, in this land of Corinth.
Only - grow big! Your father will look after the rest
with the help of any of the Gods who proves well-disposed.
I would like to see you, well looked-after and in your prime,   920
lording it over my enemies.
(Medea weeps)
But you - why do you dull your eyes with tears
turning your pale face away from me again?
Why are you not happy to hear what I said?

Medea:
It's nothing: just worrying about the children ...

Jason:
Cheer up then - I'll look after them well.

Medea:
All right. I don't doubt your words -
but woman, the female, is a creature born for tears.

Jason:
Well why, poor girl, do you weep for these children?

Medea:
I gave them birth. When you prayed for them to live their life   930
I felt pity wondering if this would come about ...
What you came to hear concerning my own situation
has been mostly said; I'll remind you of the rest ...
Since the King has decided to send me out of the country
(and no doubt it's best for me - I now clearly see -
not to stay in your way and in that of the rulers here
since I appear hostile to their house)
I am heading into exile
but how I wish the children could be reared by your hand!
Ask Creon that they not be banished.   940

Jason:
I'm not sure if I'll succeed but I ought to give it a try ...

Medea:
Get your wife to ask it of her father
that the children not be driven from here.

Jason:
All right! and I think I can persuade her.

Medea:
If she's a woman like other women, you can!

I'll even help you in this venture -
I'll send her presents far more beautiful
than any now in human hands (I'm certain of it)
- a fine robe and a wreath of gold -
with our children to carry them. So, as quickly as possible   950
let a servant go and bring the ornaments here.
(Exit Servant)
She will have not one but ten thousand blessings:
she'll get in you the best of men as a lover
and own a dress which the Sun God -
my father's father - once gave to his own offspring.
(Enter Servant carrying the robe and wreath)
Children, take this dowry in your arms, carry it
and give it to the happy Princess-bride.
She will receive no commonplace present.

Jason:

But why - foolish girl! - would you deprive yourself of these?
You hardly imagine that the palace is short of robes   960
or of gold? Hold onto these things - don't give them away.
If my bride has any regard for me
she will put me before possessions - this I know.

Medea:

Don't you believe it! They say gifts can persuade even the Gods
and gold counts for more with people than ten thousand words.
Fortune is hers; now a God adds-in these gifts.
Remember,
this girl is Queen! To spare my children from banishment
I would exchange not only gold but my very life.
So, children, make your way into that rich palace
to your father's new wife, my Queen,   970
and beg her, beseech her, not to be sent into exile -
even as you hand her my present. It's vital
that she should take these gifts into her own hands.
Go right away and when you have succeeded
bring the good news I long-for back to your mother.

Chorus:

Now I no longer have hope for the children's lives.
Already they are heading to a murder
and the bride will lay hold of the golden wreath
lay hold, unfortunate girl, of her own destruction.

She will place with her two hands   980
the ornament of Hades on her own blonde head.

The glamour, the unearthly shimmer of the robe will compel her
to try it on - so will the wreath of gold.
She will dress herself as a bride for the Underworld!
That is the trap she will fall-into
- the fate, unfortunate woman, of death. Annihilation.
She will not escape.
And you, poor wretch, unlucky bridegroom-
through your royal marriage
unknowingly you bring destruction on your children   990
and on your wife
- a horrible death.
Unhappy man, so wrong about your destiny!

I also lament for your suffering,
unfortunate mother of the children
- for you who will murder your own offspring
all because of that marriage bed
which your husband unjustly deserted   1000
to live with another bedmate.
(Enter the Tutor and children)
Tutor:
Mistress, your sons are reprieved from banishment!
and the Princess gladly received your presents into her hands.
Out of this will come reconciliation with the children.
But what's wrong?
Why, when you're in such luck, do you stand there stunned?
Why do you turn your face away from me again
and show no delight at my news?
Medea:
No! no!
Tutor:
My message doesn't call for that reaction !
Medea:
Oh misery, misery!
Tutor:
Can I have brought some bad news that I don't understand ?
Am I wrong in thinking the message was good   1010

Medea:

I don't blame *you*: you only said what you said.

Tutor:

Why do you look downhearted? Why are you crying?

Medea:

For every reason, old man! The Gods have contrived all this
- and I with my evil intentions.

Tutor:

Cheer up. Your children may yet save you from exile.

Medea:

Alas, I'll bring down others before that!

Tutor:

You are not the only one to be separated from your offspring.
We who are human must make light of suffering.

Medea:

And so I shall. But let you go inside
and prepare whatever my children need for this day.   1020
(*Exit Tutor*)
O children, children! both of you have a city
and a house where you will live when you leave wretched me,
deprived of your mother forever.
For my part, I shall go in exile to another country
before I can enjoy you both and see you happy;
before I shall have decked-out your wives and marriage-beds
or carried the torch for your wedding.
How miserable I am in my obstinacy!
I reared you, children, for nothing.
I worked, wore myself out with hardship - for nothing   1030
having put up with the cruel pains of childbirth.
Unhappy indeed - I once had many hopes both for yourselves
and that you would mind me in my old age,
and lay me out properly with your own hands when I died
- something anyone would wish. That's finished, now,
that sweet thought. Without you two
I shall lead a sad life, a life of misery.
You will not watch-over your mother with loving eyes
after you've gone away to a new life.
No, no! why are you looking at me now my pets?   1040
Why do you smile this last smile?
Aaaah - what will I do? I haven't the heart,

Women, when I see their bright glances.
I cannot do it! Never mind my previous intentions -
I will bring my sons away from this land.
Why should I afflict the father of these children with suffering
and give myself, already grieving, twice as much pain?
Not at all! Not I. Goodbye to my plans!
And yet - what's wrong with me? Do I wish to be a laughing-stock
for allowing my enemies to escape unpunished?   1050
I must go ahead with all this. It's nothing but cowardice on my part
to betray my resolution with soft words!
Get into the house, children!
(The children do not go, seeing her hesitate)
Whoever may feel
it's not right to be present at this sacrifice by me
may look to it - but I will not let my hand hesitate.
Ah!
Ah no!
My heart don't, you mustn't carry this out!
Miserable creature! Leave them alone. Spare your children.
Living with you in Athens they will make you happy ...
No! by the accursed demons in Hades   1060
never shall it happen that I'll hand over
these children for my enemies to humiliate.
That is certain. She shall not escape !
In fact my wreath is now on her head, and the royal bride
destroyed inside my robe - I can sense it!
So, I shall travel a very terrible journey
and send these children on an even more terrible one.
I want to speak to my sons.
Give me, my babies,
give your mother your right hand to kiss.   1070
O dearest hand! Mouth that I love most of all !
That look ! O handsome faces of my sons -
be happy elsewhere: what was here, your father
took away. O sweet embrace,
soft skin, ah sweetest breath of my children ...
Away, go away! I'm no longer able to look
at you both. Evil overwhelms me.
(Children leave)
Indeed I'm only beginning to understand what terrors I intend,

because my emotion is stronger than my reason
- the very cause of the worst human miseries. 1080
Chorus:
Many a time in the past
have I gone through more and more subtle reasoning
only to arrive at greater contradictions than
the female race should have to explain ...
Nevertheless we women have our own Muse
who stays with us in the search for wisdom.
Not with *all* of us: with a small number -
but perhaps you may find among the many
a few who do not lack such inspiration.
I tell you also that mortals who 1090
remain virginal, who do not have children,
are nearer to happiness
than those who become parents.
Those who are still childless, through inexperience -
not knowing whether their offspring would turn out to be
a source of joy or of sorrow, by having no children
avoid many problems.
Then again, I know that those who enjoy the sweeter growing-up
of children in their home
are worn with worry all the time. 1100
For a start: how may they rear these children well,
how leave them a livelihood?
Then - apart from all that - it is still not clear
whether they are wearing themselves out for
worthless human beings or for good.
And I shall mention a final misery,
the worst of all for any human being:
they may indeed have discovered a sufficient livelihood
and their children may be in their prime
and useful citizens ... but if destiny so decree it
then off goes foul Death carrying the children's bodies
down into Hades! 1110
What good is it all if, in addition to everything else,
the Gods inflict on mortals
this most bitter of griefs?
Medea:
Friends, I have waited a long time

anxious to find-out what will happen next over there
and now I see one of Jason's attendants
on the way. He's panting, out of breath,
which shows he has word of some new and terrible happening.   1120
(Enter Messenger)

Messenger:
O Medea! who have perpetrated a horrible, an
unnatural act, run, run! don't pass any ship
or waggon that would carry you away!

Medea:
Why ? What has happened to make me take such flight?

Messenger:
She's dead! The girl just now a Princess! Dead.
and so is Creon her father - because of your poisons.

Medea:
You have spoken the sweetest word! From now on
you shall be among my trusted workers and friends!

Messenger:
What are you saying? Woman, are you out of your mind,
        mad -
you who have destroyed the Royal House? Are you delighted   1130
to hear that? Are you not terrified at such news?

Medea:
I could give you an answer
to your question! But don't rush-away, my friend -
tell me how they were killed. If they died horribly
I would be twice as pleased.

Messenger:
When those two children of yours arrived
and entered the bridal halls with their father
we servants who had been depressed at your misfortunes
cheered-up - and straightway a rumour circulated round the palace
that you and your husband had
made-up after your former quarrel.   1140
One of us kissed the hand, another the yellow hair
of the children. I myself in delight
went with them to the women's quarters.
Our mistress - she whom we now honoured in your place -
gave Jason a look of longing
before she noticed your two sons.

At that, she immediately veiled her eyes
and turned her white neck away again,
disgusted at the children's going there. Your husband
began to placate the young girl's annoyance and spite   1150
saying, "Now don't be hostile to your friends!
Put an end to this anger, look at us again,
and consider as friends those whom your husband does.
Accept their presents and beg your father
to repeal the exile of these children - for my sake!"
Well, when she noticed the dress she could not restrain herself
but gave-in to her man's request. And before your sons
and their father had gone far from the palace
out she takes the embroidered dress and puts it on.
Settling the golden wreath on her curls as well,   1160
she arranges her hair by a bright mirror,
smiling to the ghostly image of herself.
Then she stands up from her seat and walks around inside
stepping gracefully on white, white feet,
overjoyed with her presents. Many a time
she admires herself, takes back-glances at her straightened ankle.
Then suddenly - a sight awful to behold! -
she changes colour, she staggers sideways
and, shaking in every limb barely makes it back
to collapse in her chair instead of on the ground.   1170
Some old servant, thinking that her seizure
has come from Pan or from some of the Gods
raises a cheerful cry - until he sees white froth
ooze from her mouth, the girl's eyes rolling
the blood all drained from her skin ...
Then the servant gives a shriek of the opposite kind -
a great cry of mourning and immediately heads to the father's
                    quarters;
another runs for her husband
to tell him of his bride's mishap - and the whole building
begins to resound with non-stop dashing-around ...   1180
(All this in the time a quick runner would have passed the turn
and be nearing the full length of a track.)
Then she, poor girl, wakes from that silence, eyes shut tight,
and gives a horrible scream -
because now she is being tormented, twice over .

For a start, the golden wreath on her head
sends out an amazing stream of devouring flame;
and then the fine robe - your children's gift -
begins to torture the poor girl's delicate flesh.
She gets up from her chair and runs around, on fire !   1190
shaking her hair, her head, this way and that
trying to knock the wreath off. But the gold crown
holds tight, unshakeable, and whenever she tosses her hair
fire blazes-up twice as much.
Overcome with agony, she falls to the floor,
totally unrecognisable unless to her own father.
Nor could the former beauty of her eyes be seen
nor her lovely face: blood drips from the crown
of her head, glowing with fire.
Like drops from a pine, flesh begins to fall off her bones -   1200
savaged by the hidden jaws of poison.
A shocking sight! We were all terrified of touching
her corpse: we had her fate as a warning!
Her unfortunate father however, ignorant of the horror,
suddenly enters the room and falls on her corpse.
Immediately he starts lamenting, clasping her body,
kissing her, screaming, "O my unfortunate girl,
which of the Gods destroyed you so shamelessly?
Which of them leaves me here, child, like an old tomb,
bereft of you? If only I could die along with you!"   1210
When he has finished weeping and shouting
the old man goes to raise-up his aged body
- but it sticks, like ivy to laurel branches,
to her filmy clothes! A ghastly struggle -
because he's trying to lift his knee while
she holds him back. When he
attempts to force himself upright
she tears the old flesh from his bones. . .
Finally, his life is snuffed-out. The unfortunate man
gives up the ghost, unable to take any more punishment.
Now child and aged father lie, two corpses,   1220
side-by-side - a tragedy to be mourned-for only with tears.
As to your part in all this: let that remain unspoken-
you will, yourself, know best how to escape punishment.

Not for the first time now do I see human life as a shadow
nor would I be afraid to say that those mortals who seem clever,
knowledgeable with their theories, and all that.
- that they're the most foolish of all
because no human being is happy at heart.
When money is plentiful maybe one person might emerge
luckier than another - but happy, no!   1230
Chorus:
  It seems that Fate has today
  justly brought much evil on Jason.
  Poor girl! how we pity you for your misfortune,
  daughter of Creon, gone to your palace in Hades
  because of your marriage to Jason.
Medea:
  Friends, I've made my decision: without any delay
  to kill my children, then get out of the country
  - and not, by hesitating, hand them over
  for someone else to murder with a more brutal hand.
  For every reason, they have to die. Since this must be   1240
  I, who gave them birth, will kill them.
  Steel yourself my heart! Why do I hesitate
  to carry-out this awful, necessary, evil?
  Come, wretched hand of mine, take up the sword!
  Take it. Crawl towards this sad beginning of another life
  and don't be cowardly, don't think about your sons -
  how very dear they are, how you gave them birth. No!
  for this short day forget about your children.
  Mourn for them afterwards - because even though you kill them
  still they are beloved. Unfortunate woman !
  (Exit Medea)
Chorus:
  O Earth and resplendent
  ray of the Sun, look, look down on this
  destructive woman before she lays bloody hands
  on her children, killing her own -
  for she sprang from your golden lineage and it is not right
  that people who came from a God
  should die at the hands of mortals.
  Prevent her, Apollo born of Zeus,
  stop her! Banish from the house

this wretched, this murderous Fury driven by revenge.   1260
In vain, wasted, were the birth-pains for your offspring,
truly in vain did you bear your beloved children.
O woman who even passed through the blue rocks of the
        Symplegades
- that most unfriendly of straits - o wretched woman,
why, why does this heavy anger weigh on your mind?
Why must it be foul murder
that settles it ?
It is a grievous thing for mortals when
the blood of their relatives is spilt on the earth. I know
that punishment for infanticide falls on their house from Zeus.   1270
(Children cry, off-stage)

Child 1:

Oh what can I do? Where can I escape my mother's hands?

Child 2:

I don't know, dearest brother. We're finished!

Chorus:

Do you hear, do you hear it? The cry of children!
No you wretched, you doomed woman. No!
Shall I go into the house? To prevent the murder
of the children is my duty ...
(Chorus beats at the door)

Child 1:

Please, by the Gods, help us! We need help!

Child 2:

We are almost within reach of her sword!

Chorus:

Monster! are you really made of stone, of iron,
that you would kill the offspring you bore,   1280
with your very own hand as the instrument?
I have only heard of one woman of old - one! -
who laid hands on her dear children:
Ino, driven mad by the Gods when the wife of Zeus
sent her, demented from her home.
She, poor wretch, for the impious
murder of her offspring, fell into the sea
- stepping with her foot out from the cliff -
and perished, dying along with her two children.
What could be worse than that ?   1290

O marriage-bed, fraught with suffering for women,
how many evils have you brought on mortals!
(Enter Jason)
Jason:
You women, who stand near this house -
is the one who did those horrible things, inside
- Medea - or has she run away?
She'll have to hide herself under the earth,
or raise her body on wings up into the air,
to escape the vengence of the Royal House !
Does she imagine that, having murdered the rulers of the land,
she will herself get away from here unharmed?   1300
Anyway, I don't care about her but about my sons.
Those she wronged will punish her -
but I have come to save the lives of my children
for fear that the King's relations may do them harm
in avenging that wicked murder by their mother.
Chorus:
Unfortunate man! You don't realise what evil you have come-upon,
Jason, or you would not have spoken those words!
Jason:
What is it? Does she wish to kill me too?
Chorus:
Your children are dead by their mother's hand !
Jason:
No! no! What are you saying? Woman, you have destroyed me!   1310
Chorus:
Think of your children as no longer alive.
Jason:
Where did she kill them? Inside, outside the house?
Chorus:
(Pointing) Open the doors and you'll see the corpses of your sons.
Jason:
Servants, smash the bolts immediately!
Knock off the hinges, let me see this double horror,
the dead pair, and the woman I will kill in revenge!
(Medea appears above the roof in a chariot drawn by dragons)
Medea:
Why do you rattle and unbar these doors?
To see the bodies? To see me who did it?

Give up your efforts! If you want something
say what you want - but you'll never lay a hand on me!   1320
Helios the Sun, my father's father, gives me this chariot
for protection against any enemy hand.

Jason:

O thing hated, O woman absolutely the most detested
by the Gods, by me, by all the human race!
You dared to stick a sword in your own children,
you, their mother! You destroyed me, left me childless ...
After doing all that, how can you look at the sun,
at the earth - after daring this most impious of all acts?
May you be wiped-out! Now I can see - but I was mad then
when I brought you out of a barbarian house and country   1330
into a Greek home . You, pure evil !
a traitor to your father, to the land that reared you.
The Gods have cursed me with your curse
because you killed your brother at the family hearth,
then boarded the sweet Argo ...
But that was only the start! after you married
myself here and bore me sons
you murdered them! All over sex, over a bedmate!
No Greek woman ever dared do that -
and yet I thought fit to marry you before any of them   1340
- a marriage both hateful and destructive for me -
to marry you, a lioness, no woman! with a nature more savage
than that of Tyrrhenian Scylla.
But I could not disturb *you* with ten thousand insults
- you have such ruthlessness in your nature.
Go away, pervert, defiled with the blood of your own children!
I only want to lament my destiny.
I will neither enjoy my new marriage now
nor have the children I fathered and reared
alive to talk to. I am finished.   1350

Medea:

I would make a long reply to these remarks
if Father Zeus did not know
the services you had from me and how you paid them back.
Having dishonoured my bed, you were not going
To lead an enjoyable life and laugh at me!
Neither could your Princess, nor Creon who suggested the marriage

expel me from this land and get away with it!
So my reply is: call me lioness if you like,
or even Scylla of the Tyrrhenian shore
but I have strangled your heart and rightly so!   1360
Jason:
Yes but you grieve too! You share my sufferings ...
Medea:
You are right - but it lessens the sadness if you cannot mock.
Jason:
O my sons, what a wicked mother you had!
Medea:
O my children, you were destroyed by your father's vice!
Jason:
It was no hand of mine that murdered them.
Medea:
No - only your pride and your new relationship.
Jason:
So you thought it worth while to murder them over sex?
Medea:
Do you really imagine that such misery does not matter to a woman?
Jason:
To a chaste woman, no; but it's the only evil for *you!*
Medea:
They are no longer alive - that's what will torture *you!*   1370
Jason:
They are alive all right - alas - as avengers on your head.
Medea:
The Gods know who started all this misery.
Jason:
Yes they *do* know - about your sick mind!
Medea:
Go on, hate me! I loathe your bitter voice.
Jason:
And I yours! To separate is easy.
Medea:
Well then, what is your request? I too want only to leave.
Jason:
Hand me over the corpses to bury and to lament.
Medea:
Never! I shall bury them with my own hand

after carrying them to the sanctuary of Hera Akraia
so that no enemy may dishonour them
by digging-up their graves; and in the land of Sisyphus, Corinth   1380
I'll set-up a solemn festival and ceremony
from now on, in atonement for this impious murder.
I shall go myself, to Athens, land of Erechtheus
and live with Aegeus, son of Pandion.
You who are evil shall, as is fitting, die an evil death
- struck on the head by wreckage from the Argo,
after you've known the bitter end to marrying me.

Jason:

May a Fury destroy you, for those children!
and Justice, who avenges murder.   1390

Medea:

Who listens to you - does any God or spirit?
- you perjurer, you betrayer of a visitor.

Jason:

You, you foul bitch, you child-killer!

Medea:

Off with you into the palace and bury your bride!

Jason:

I am going, having lost my two children.

Medea:

You are not really in mourning yet - wait until you're old!

Jason:

O children most beloved -

Medea:

- By their mother - not by you!

Jason:

Then why did you kill them?

Medea:

To finish you off !

Jason:

How I would love, in this misfortune,
only to kiss my sons' dear mouths ...   1400

Medea:

Now you call for them! Now you would kiss them -
who lately rejected them.

Jason:

Allow me, for the Gods' sake,

to touch the soft skin of my children!
Medea:
No! You are wasting your breath.
Jason:
Zeus, do you hear how I am being got rid of
and what I suffer from this atrocious woman,
this childkiller, this lioness?
Nevertheless I shall do what I can -
I shall mourn and call-on the Gods to witness   1410
that you killed my children and that you prevent me
from touching their hands or burying their bodies.
I wish I never had had them
rather than see them wiped-out by you.
(Medea disappears, the chariot drawing her out of sight)
Chorus:
Much is determined by Olympian Zeus,
much that is unlooked-for the Gods bring about
and what we expected does not come to pass.
Zeus finds a way to cause the unforeseen.
And so it happened in this case.   1420

ΕΥΡΙΠΙΔΟΥ ΜΗΔΕΙΑ.

ΤΡΟΦΟΣ.

Εἴθ᾽ ὤφελ᾽ Ἀργοῦς μὴ διαπτάσθαι σκάφος
Κόλχων ἐς αἶαν κυανέας Συμπληγάδας,
μηδ᾽ ἐν νάπαισι Πηλίου πεσεῖν ποτε
τμηθεῖσα πεύκη, μηδ᾽ ἐρετμῶσαι χέρας
ἀνδρῶν ἀριστέων, οἳ τὸ πάγχρυσον δέρος   5
Πελίᾳ μετῆλθον. οὐ γὰρ ἂν δέσποιν᾽ ἐμὴ
Μήδεια πύργους γῆς ἔπλευσ᾽ Ἰωλκίας
ἔρωτι θυμὸν ἐκπλαγεῖσ᾽ Ἰάσονος,
οὐδ᾽ ἂν κτανεῖν πείσασα Πελιάδας κόρας
πατέρα κατῴκει τήνδε γῆν Κορινθίαν   10
σὺν ἀνδρὶ καὶ τέκνοισιν, ἀνδάνουσα μὲν
φυγῇ πολιτῶν ὧν ἀφίκετο χθόνα
αὐτή τε πάντα συμφέρουσ᾽ Ἰάσονι—
ἥπερ μεγίστη γίγνεται σωτηρία,
ὅταν γυνὴ πρὸς ἄνδρα μὴ διχοστατῇ—   15
νῦν δ᾽ ἐχθρὰ πάντα, καὶ νοσεῖ τὰ φίλτατα.
προδοὺς γὰρ αὐτοῦ τέκνα δεσπότιν τ᾽ ἐμὴν
γάμοις Ἰάσων βασιλικοῖς εὐνάζεται,
γήμας Κρέοντος παῖδ᾽, ὃς αἰσυμνᾷ χθονός·
Μήδεια δ᾽ ἡ δύστηνος ἠτιμασμένη   20
βοᾷ μὲν ὅρκους, ἀνακαλεῖ δὲ δεξιὰς,
πίστιν μεγίστην, καὶ θεοὺς μαρτύρεται
οἵας ἀμοιβῆς ἐξ Ἰάσονος κυρεῖ.
κεῖται δ᾽ ἄσιτος, σῶμ᾽ ὑφεῖσ᾽ ἀλγηδόσι
τὸν πάντα συντήκουσα δακρύοις χρόνον   25
ἐπεὶ πρὸς ἀνδρὸς ᾔσθετ᾽ ἠδικημένη,
οὔτ᾽ ὄμμ᾽ ἐπαίρουσ᾽ οὔτ᾽ ἀπαλλάσσουσα γῆς
πρόσωπον· ὡς δὲ πέτρος ἢ θαλάσσιος
κλύδων ἀκούει νουθετουμένη φίλων·
πλὴν εἴ ποτε στρέψασα πάλλευκον δέρην   30
αὐτὴ πρὸς αὑτὴν πατέρ᾽ ἀποιμώζει φίλον
καὶ γαῖαν οἴκους θ᾽, οὓς προδοῦσ᾽ ἀφίκετο
μετ᾽ ἀνδρὸς ὅς σφε νῦν ἀτιμάσας ἔχει.
ἔγνωκε δ᾽ ἡ τάλαινα συμφορᾶς ὕπο
οἷον πατρῴας μὴ ἀπολείπεσθαι χθονός.   35
στυγεῖ δὲ παῖδας οὐδ᾽ ὁρῶσ᾽ εὐφραίνεται.
δέδοικα δ᾽ αὐτὴν μή τι βουλεύσῃ νέον·
δεινὴ γάρ· οὔτοι ῥᾳδίως γε συμβαλὼν
ἔχθραν τις αὐτῇ καλλίνικον οἴσεται.
ἀλλ᾽ οἵδε παῖδες ἐκ τρόχων πεπαυμένοι   45

στείχουσι, μητρὸς οὐδὲν ἐννοούμενοι
κακῶν· νέα γὰρ φροντὶς οὐκ ἀλγεῖν φιλεῖ.

ΠΑΙΔΑΓΩΓΟΣ.

παλαιὸν οἴκων κτῆμα δεσποίνης ἐμῆς,
τί πρὸς πύλαισι τήνδ' ἄγουσ' ἐρημίαν　　　　　50
ἔστηκας, αὐτὴ θρεομένη σαυτῇ κακά ;
πῶς σοῦ μόνη Μήδεια λείπεσθαι θέλει ;
ΤΡ.　τέκνων ὀπαδὲ πρέσβυ τῶν Ἰάσονος,
χρηστοῖσι δούλοις συμφορὰ τὰ δεσποτῶν
κακῶς πίτνοντα καὶ φρενῶν ἀνθάπτεται.　　　55
ἐγὼ γὰρ ἐς τοῦτ' ἐκβέβηκ' ἀλγηδόνος,
ὥσθ' ἵμερός μ' ὑπῆλθε γῇ τε κοὐρανῷ
λέξαι μολούσῃ δεῦρο δεσποίνης τύχας.
ΠΑΙ.　οὔπω γὰρ ἡ τάλαινα παύεται γόων ;
ΤΡ.　ζηλῶ σ'· ἐν ἀρχῇ πῆμα κοὐδέπω μεσοῖ.　　60
ΠΑΙ.　ὦ μῶρος, εἰ χρὴ δεσπότας εἰπεῖν τόδε·
ὡς οὐδὲν οἶδε τῶν νεωτέρων κακῶν.
ΤΡ.　τί δ' ἔστιν, ὦ γεραιέ ; μὴ φθόνει φράσαι.
ΠΑΙ.　οὐδέν· μετέγνων καὶ τὰ πρόσθ' εἰρημένα.
ΤΡ.　μή, πρὸς γενείου, κρύπτε σύνδουλον σέθεν·　　65
σιγὴν γάρ, εἰ χρή, τῶνδε θήσομαι πέρι.
ΠΑΙ.　ἤκουσά του λέγοντος οὐ δοκῶν κλύειν,
πεσσοὺς προσελθών, ἔνθα δὴ παλαίτεροι
θάσσουσι, σεμνὸν ἀμφὶ Πειρήνης ὕδωρ,
ὡς τούσδε παῖδας γῆς ἐλᾶν Κορινθίας　　　70
σὺν μητρὶ μέλλοι τῆσδε κοίρανος χθονὸς
Κρέων. ὁ μέντοι μῦθος εἰ σαφὴς ὅδε
οὐκ οἶδα· βουλοίμην δ' ἂν οὐκ εἶναι τόδε.
ΤΡ.　καὶ ταῦτ' Ἰάσων παῖδας ἐξανέξεται
πάσχοντας, εἰ καὶ μητρὶ διαφορὰν ἔχει ;　　75
ΠΑΙ.　παλαιὰ καινῶν λείπεται κηδευμάτων,
κοὐκ ἔστ' ἐκεῖνος τοῖσδε δώμασιν φίλος.
ΤΡ.　ἀπωλόμεσθ' ἄρ', εἰ κακὸν προσοίσομεν
νέον παλαιῷ, πρὶν τόδ' ἐξηντληκέναι.
ΠΑΙ.　ἀτὰρ σύ γ'—οὐ γὰρ καιρὸς εἰδέναι τόδε　　80
δέσποιναν—ἡσύχαζε καὶ σίγα λόγον.
ΤΡ.　ὦ τέκν', ἀκούεθ' οἷος εἰς ὑμᾶς πατήρ ;
ὄλοιτο μὲν μή· δεσπότης γάρ ἐστ' ἐμός·
ἀτὰρ κακός γ' ὢν ἐς φίλους ἁλίσκεται.
ΠΑΙ.　τίς δ' οὐχὶ θνητῶν ; ἄρτι γιγνώσκεις τόδε,　　85
ὡς πᾶς τις αὑτὸν τοῦ πέλας μᾶλλον φιλεῖ,
οἱ μὲν δικαίως, οἱ δὲ καὶ κέρδους χάριν,
εἰ τούσδε γ' εὐνῆς εἵνεκ' οὐ στέργει πατήρ.
ΤΡ.　ἴτ'· εὖ γὰρ ἔσται δωμάτων ἔσω, τέκνα.
σὺ δ' ὡς μάλιστα τούσδ' ἐρημώσας ἔχε　　　90

καὶ μὴ πέλαζε μητρὶ δυσθυμουμένῃ.
ἤδη γὰρ εἶδον ὄμμα νιν ταυρουμένην
τοῖσδ', ὥς τι δρασείουσαν· οὐδὲ παύσεται
χόλου, σάφ' οἶδα, πρὶν κατασκῆψαί τινα.
ἐχθρούς γε μέντοι, μὴ φίλους, δράσειέ τι.   95

ΜΗΔΕΙΑ.

ἰώ,
δύστανος ἐγὼ μελέα τε πόνων,
ἰώ μοί μοι, πῶς ἂν ὀλοίμαν;
ΤΡ. τόδ' ἐκεῖνο, φίλοι παῖδες· μήτηρ
κινεῖ κραδίαν, κινεῖ δὲ χόλον.
σπεύδετε θᾶσσον δώματος εἴσω   100
καὶ μὴ πελάσητ' ὄμματος ἐγγὺς
μηδὲ προσέλθητ', ἀλλὰ φυλάσσεσθ'
ἄγριον ἦθος στυγεράν τε φύσιν
φρενὸς αὐθάδους.
ἴτε νῦν χωρεῖθ' ὡς τάχος εἴσω.   105
δῆλον δ' ἀρχῆς ἐξαιρόμενον
νέφος οἰμωγῆς ὡς τάχ' ἀνάψει
μείζονι θυμῷ· τί ποτ' ἐργάσεται
μεγαλόσπλαγχνος δυσκατάπαυστος
ψυχὴ δηχθεῖσα κακοῖσιν;   110
ΜΗ. αἰαῖ,
ἔπαθον τλάμων ἔπαθον μεγάλων
ἄξι' ὀδυρμῶν· ὦ κατάρατοι
παῖδες ὄλοισθε στυγερᾶς ματρὸς
σὺν πατρί, καὶ πᾶς δόμος ἔρροι.
ΤΡ. ἰώ μοί μοι, ἰὼ τλήμων·   115
τί δέ σοι παῖδες πατρὸς ἀμπλακίας
μετέχουσι; τί τούσδ' ἔχθεις; οἴμοι,
τέκνα, μή τι πάθηθ' ὡς ὑπεραλγῶ.
δεινὰ τυράννων λήματα καί πως
ὀλίγ' ἀρχόμενοι, πολλὰ κρατοῦντες   120
χαλεπῶς ὀργὰς μεταβάλλουσιν.
τὸ γὰρ εἰθίσθαι ζῆν ἐπ' ἴσοισιν
κρεῖσσον· ἐμοὶ γοῦν ἐπὶ μὴ μεγάλοις
ὀχυρῶς εἴη καταγηράσκειν.
τῶν γὰρ μετρίων πρῶτα μὲν εἰπεῖν   125
τοὔνομα νικᾷ, χρῆσθαί τε μακρῷ
λῷστα βροτοῖσιν· τὰ δ' ὑπερβάλλοντ'
οὐδένα καιρὸν [δύναται θνητοῖς]
μείζους δ' ἄτας, ὅταν ὀργισθῇ
δαίμων οἴκοις, ἀπέδωκεν.   130

ΧΟΡΟΣ.

ἔκλυον φωνάν, ἔκλυον δὲ βοὰν
τᾶς δυστάνου Κολχίδος. οὐδέ πω
ἤπιος; ἀλλ᾽, ὦ γεραιά, λέξον·
ἐπ᾽ ἀμφιπύλου γὰρ ἔσω μελάθρου βοὰν   135
ἔκλυον, οὐδὲ συνήδομαι, ὦ γύναι,
ἄλγεσι δώματος· εἰπέ, τί μοι, φίλα, κέκρανται;

ΤΡ.   οὐκ εἰσὶ δόμοι· φροῦδα τάδ᾽ ἤδη.
τὸν μὲν γὰρ ἔχει λέκτρα τυράννων,   140
ἣ δ᾽ ἐν θαλάμοις τήκει βιοτὴν
δέσποινα, φίλων οὐδενὸς οὐδὲν
παραθαλπομένη φρένα μύθοις.

ΜΗ.   αἰαῖ,
διά μου κεφαλᾶς φλὸξ οὐρανία
βαίη· τί δέ μοι ζῆν ἔτι κέρδος;   145
φεῦ φεῦ· θανάτῳ καταλυσαίμαν
βιοτὰν στυγερὰν προλιποῦσα.

ΧΟ.   ἄιες, ὦ Ζεῦ καὶ γᾶ καὶ φῶς,
ἰαχὰν οἵαν ἁ δύστανος
μέλπει νύμφα;   150
τίς σοί ποτε τᾶς ἀπλάτου
κοίτας ἔρος, ὦ ματαία;
σπεύσει θανάτου τελευτά·
μηδὲν τόδε λίσσου.
εἰ δὲ σὸς πόσις   155
καινὰ λέχη σεβίζει,
κοινὸν τόδε· μὴ χαράσσου·
Ζεύς σοι τάδε συνδικήσει. μὴ λίαν
τάκου δυρομένα σὸν εὐνάταν.

ΜΗ.   ὦ μεγάλα Θέμι καὶ πότνι᾽ Ἄρτεμι†   160
λεύσσεθ᾽ ἃ πάσχω, μεγάλοις ὅρκοις
ἐνδησαμένα τὸν κατάρατον
πόσιν, ὅν ποτ᾽ ἐγὼ νύμφαν τ᾽ ἐσίδοιμ᾽
αὐτοῖς μελάθροις διακναιομένους,
οἵ γ᾽ ἐμὲ πρόσθεν τολμῶσ᾽ ἀδικεῖν.   165
ὦ πάτερ, ὦ πόλις, ὧν ἀπενάσθην
αἰσχρῶς τὸν ἐμὸν κτείνασα κάσιν.

ΤΡ.   κλύεθ᾽ οἷα λέγει κἀπιβοᾶται
Θέμιν εὐκταίαν Ζῆνά θ᾽, ὃς ὅρκων
θνητοῖς ταμίας νενόμισται.   170
οὐκ ἔστιν ὅπως ἔν τινι μικρῷ
δέσποινα χόλον καταπαύσει.

ΧΟ.   πῶς ἂν ἐς ὄψιν τὰν ἀμετέραν
ἔλθοι μύθων τ᾽ αὐδαθέντων
δέξαιτ᾽ ὀμφάν,   175
εἴ πως βαρύθυμον ὀργὰν

καὶ λῆμα φρενῶν μεθείη;
μήτοι τό γ᾽ ἐμὸν πρόθυμον
φίλοισιν ἀπέστω.
ἀλλὰ βᾶσά νιν   180
δεῦρο πόρευσον οἴκων
ἔξω, φίλα, εἰ τάδ᾽ αὐδᾷ·
σπεῦσον πρίν τι κακῶσαι τοὺς εἴσω·
πένθος γὰρ μεγάλως τόδ᾽ ὁρμᾶται.

ΤΡ.   δράσω τάδ᾽· ἀτὰρ φόβος εἰ πείσω·
[δέσποιναν ἐμήν·]   185
μόχθου δὲ χάριν τήνδ᾽ ἐπιδώσω.
καίτοι τοκάδος δέργμα λεαίνης
ἀποταυροῦται δμωσίν, ὅταν τις
μῦθον προφέρων πέλας ὁρμηθῇ.
σκαιοὺς δὲ λέγων κοὐδέν τι σοφοὺς   190
τοὺς πρόσθε βροτοὺς οὐκ ἂν ἁμάρτοις,
οἵτινες ὕμνους ἐπὶ μὲν θαλίαις
ἐπί τ᾽ εἰλαπίναις καὶ παρὰ δείπνοις
ηὕροντο βίου τερπνὰς ἀκοάς·
στυγίους δὲ βροτῶν οὐδεὶς λύπας   195
ηὕρετο μούσῃ καὶ πολυχόρδοις
ᾠδαῖς παύειν, ἐξ ὧν θάνατοι
δειναί τε τύχαι σφάλλουσι δόμους.
καίτοι τάδε μὲν κέρδος ἀκεῖσθαι
μολπαῖσι βροτούς· ἵνα δ᾽ εὔδειπνοι   200
δαῖτες, τί μάτην τείνουσι βοήν;
τὸ παρὸν γὰρ ἔχει τέρψιν ἀφ᾽ αὑτοῦ
δαιτὸς πλήρωμα βροτοῖσιν.

ΧΟ.   ἰαχὰν ἄιον πολύστονον γόων,
λιγυρὰ δ᾽ ἄχεα μογερὰ βοᾷ   205
τὸν ἐν λέχει προδόταν κακόνυμφον·
θεοκλυτεῖ δ᾽ ἄδικα παθοῦσα
τὰν Ζηνὸς ὁρκίαν Θέμιν,
ἅ νιν ἔβασεν
Ἑλλάδ᾽ ἐς ἀντίπορον   210
δι᾽ ἅλα μύχιον ἐφ᾽ ἁλμυρὰν
πόντου κλῇδ᾽ ἀπέραντον.

ΜΗ.   Κορίνθιαι γυναῖκες, ἐξῆλθον δόμων,
μή μοί τι μέμφησθ᾽· οἶδα γὰρ πολλοὺς βροτῶν   215
σεμνοὺς γεγῶτας, τοὺς μὲν ὀμμάτων ἄπο,
τοὺς δ᾽ ἐν θυραίοις. οἱ δ᾽ ἀφ᾽ ἡσύχου ποδὸς
δύσκλειαν ἐκτήσαντο καὶ ῥαθυμίαν.
δίκη γὰρ οὐκ ἔνεστιν ὀφθαλμοῖς βροτῶν,
ὅστις πρὶν ἀνδρὸς σπλάγχνον ἐκμαθεῖν σαφῶς   220
στυγεῖ δεδορκώς, οὐδὲν ἠδικημένος.

χρὴ δὲ ξένον μὲν κάρτα προσχωρεῖν πόλει·
οὐδ᾽ ἀστὸν ᾔνεσ᾽ ὅστις αὐθάδης γεγὼς
πικρὸς πολίταις ἐστὶν ἀμαθίας ὕπο.
ἐμοὶ δ᾽ ἄελπτον πρᾶγμα προσπεσὸν τόδε   225
ψυχὴν διέφθαρκ᾽· οἴχομαι δὲ καὶ βίου
χάριν μεθεῖσα κατθανεῖν χρῄζω, φίλαι.
ἐν ᾧ γὰρ ἦν μοι πάντα γιγνώσκειν καλῶς,
κάκιστος ἀνδρῶν ἐκβέβηχ᾽ οὑμὸς πόσις.
πάντων δ᾽ ὅσ᾽ ἔστ᾽ ἔμψυχα καὶ γνώμην ἔχει   230
γυναῖκές ἐσμεν ἀθλιώτατον φυτόν·
ἃς πρῶτα μὲν δεῖ χρημάτων ὑπερβολῇ
πόσιν πρίασθαι δεσπότην τε σώματος
λαβεῖν· λαβεῖν γὰρ οὐ, τόδ᾽ ἄλγιον κακόν·
κἂν τῷδ᾽ ἀγὼν μέγιστος, ἢ κακὸν λαβεῖν   235
ἢ χρηστόν. οὐ γὰρ εὐκλεεῖς ἀπαλλαγαὶ
γυναιξίν, οὐδ᾽ οἷόν τ᾽ ἀνήνασθαι πόσιν.
ἐς καινὰ δ᾽ ἤθη καὶ νόμους ἀφιγμένην
δεῖ μάντιν εἶναι, μὴ μαθοῦσαν οἴκοθεν,
ὅτῳ μάλιστα χρήσεται ξυνευνέτῃ.   240
κἂν μὲν τάδ᾽ ἡμῖν ἐκπονουμέναισιν εὖ
πόσις ξυνοικῇ μὴ βίᾳ φέρων ζυγόν,
ζηλωτὸς αἰών· εἰ δὲ μή, θανεῖν χρεών.
ἀνὴρ δ᾽, ὅταν τοῖς ἔνδον ἄχθηται ξυνών,
ἔξω μολὼν ἔπαυσε καρδίαν ἄσης·   245
ἡμῖν δ᾽ ἀνάγκη πρὸς μίαν ψυχὴν βλέπειν.   247
λέγουσι δ᾽ ἡμᾶς ὡς ἀκίνδυνον βίον
ζῶμεν κατ᾽ οἴκους, οἳ δὲ μάρνανται δορί·
κακῶς φρονοῦντες· ὡς τρὶς ἂν παρ᾽ ἀσπίδα   250
στῆναι θέλοιμ᾽ ἂν μᾶλλον ἢ τεκεῖν ἅπαξ.
ἀλλ᾽ οὐ γὰρ αὑτὸς πρὸς σὲ κἀμ᾽ ἥκει λόγος·
σοὶ μὲν πόλις θ᾽ ἥδ᾽ ἐστὶ καὶ πατρὸς δόμοι
βίου τ᾽ ὄνησις καὶ φίλων συνουσία,
ἐγὼ δ᾽ ἔρημος ἄπολις οὖσ᾽ ὑβρίζομαι   255
πρὸς ἀνδρός, ἐκ γῆς βαρβάρου λελῃσμένη,
οὐ μητέρ᾽, οὐκ ἀδελφόν, οὐχὶ συγγενῆ
μεθορμίσασθαι τῆσδ᾽ ἔχουσα συμφορᾶς.
τοσοῦτον οὖν σου τυγχάνειν βουλήσομαι,
ἤν μοι πόρος τις μηχανή τ᾽ ἐξευρεθῇ   260
πόσιν δίκην τῶνδ᾽ ἀντιτίσασθαι κακῶν,
σιγᾶν. γυνὴ γὰρ τἆλλα μὲν φόβου πλέα   263
κακή τ᾽ ἐς ἀλκὴν καὶ σίδηρον εἰσορᾶν·
ὅταν δ᾽ ἐς εὐνὴν ἠδικημένη κυρῇ,   265
οὐκ ἔστιν ἄλλη φρὴν μιαιφονωτέρα.
ΧΟ. δράσω τάδ᾽· ἐνδίκως γὰρ ἐκτίσει πόσιν,
Μήδεια. πενθεῖν δ᾽ οὔ σε θαυμάζω τύχας.
ὁρῶ δὲ καὶ Κρέοντα, τῆσδ᾽ ἄνακτα γῆς,

στείχοντα, καινῶν ἄγγελον βουλευμάτων. 270

ΚΡΕΩΝ.

σὲ τὴν σκυθρωπὸν καὶ πόσει θυμουμένην,
Μήδειαν, εἶπον τῆσδε γῆς ἔξω περᾶν
φυγάδα λαβοῦσαν δισσὰ σὺν σαυτῇ τέκνα,
καὶ μή τι μέλλειν· ὡς ἐγὼ βραβεὺς λόγου
τοῦδ' εἰμὶ κοὐκ ἄπειμι πρὸς δόμους πάλιν, 275
πρὶν ἄν σε γαίας τερμόνων ἔξω βάλω.
ΜΗ. αἰαῖ· πανώλης ἡ τάλαιν' ἀπόλλυμαι.
ἐχθροὶ γὰρ ἐξιᾶσι πάντα δὴ κάλων,
κοὐκ ἔστιν ἄτης εὐπρόσοιστος ἔκβασις.
ἐρήσομαι δὲ καὶ κακῶς πάσχουσ' ὅμως· 280
τίνος μ' ἕκατι γῆς ἀποστέλλεις, Κρέον;
ΚΡ. δέδοικά σ', οὐδὲν δεῖ παραμπέχειν λόγους,
μή μοί τι δράσῃς παῖδ' ἀνήκεστον κακόν.
συμβάλλεται δὲ πολλὰ τοῦδε δείματος·
σοφὴ πέφυκας καὶ κακῶν πολλῶν ἴδρις, 285
λυπεῖ δὲ λέκτρων ἀνδρὸς ἐστερημένη.
κλύω δ' ἀπειλεῖν σ', ὡς ἀπαγγέλλουσί μοι,
τὸν δόντα καὶ γήμαντα καὶ γαμουμένην
δράσειν τι. ταῦτ' οὖν πρὶν παθεῖν φυλάξομαι.
κρεῖσσον δέ μοι νῦν πρός σ' ἀπεχθέσθαι, γύναι, 290
ἢ μαλθακισθένθ' ὕστερον μεταστένειν.
ΜΗ. φεῦ φεῦ.
οὐ νῦν με πρῶτον, ἀλλὰ πολλάκις, Κρέον,
ἔβλαψε δόξα μεγάλα τ' εἴργασται κακά.
χρὴ δ' οὔποθ' ὅστις ἀρτίφρων πέφυκ' ἀνὴρ
παῖδας περισσῶς ἐκδιδάσκεσθαι σοφούς· 295
χωρὶς γὰρ ἄλλης ἧς ἔχουσιν ἀργίας
φθόνον πρὸς ἀστῶν ἀλφάνουσι δυσμενῆ.
σκαιοῖσι μὲν γὰρ καινὰ προσφέρων σοφὰ
δόξεις ἀχρεῖος κοὐ σοφὸς πεφυκέναι·
τῶν δ' αὖ δοκούντων εἰδέναι τι ποικίλον 300
κρείσσων νομισθεὶς λυπρὸς ἐν πόλει φανεῖ.
ἐγὼ δὲ καὐτὴ τῆσδε κοινωνῶ τύχης.
σοφὴ γὰρ οὖσα, τοῖς μέν εἰμ' ἐπίφθονος,
τοῖσδ' αὖ προσάντης εἰμὶ κοὐκ ἄγαν σοφή.
σὺ δ' αὖ φοβεῖ με μή τι πλημμελὲς πάθῃς· 305
οὐχ ὧδ' ἔχει μοι, μὴ τρέσῃς ἡμᾶς, Κρέον,
ὥστ' ἐς τυράννους ἄνδρας ἐξαμαρτάνειν.
τί γὰρ σύ μ' ἠδίκηκας; ἐξέδου κόρην
ὅτῳ σε θυμὸς ἦγεν. ἀλλ' ἐμὸν πόσιν 310
μισῶ· σὺ δ', οἶμαι, σωφρονῶν ἔδρας τάδε,
καὶ νῦν τὸ μὲν σὸν οὐ φθονῶ καλῶς ἔχειν·

νυμφεύετ᾽, εὖ πράσσοιτε· τήνδε δὲ χθόνα
ἐᾶτέ μ᾽ οἰκεῖν. καὶ γὰρ ἠδικημένοι
σιγησόμεσθα, κρεισσόνων νικώμενοι.   315

KP.   λέγεις ἀκοῦσαι μαλθάκ᾽, ἀλλ᾽ ἔσω φρενῶν
ὀρρωδία μοι μή τι βουλεύῃς κακόν,
τοσῷδε δ᾽ ἧσσον ἢ πάρος πέποιθά σοι·
γυνὴ γὰρ ὀξύθυμος, ὡς δ᾽ αὕτως ἀνήρ,
ῥᾴων φυλάσσειν ἢ σιωπηλὸς σοφός.   320
ἀλλ᾽ ἔξιθ᾽ ὡς τάχιστα, μὴ λόγους λέγε·
ὡς ταῦτ᾽ ἄραρε, κοὐκ ἔχεις τέχνην ὅπως
μενεῖς παρ᾽ ἡμῖν οὖσα δυσμενὴς ἐμοί.

MH.   μή, πρός σε γονάτων τῆς τε νεογάμου κόρης.

KP.   λόγους ἀναλοῖς· οὐ γὰρ ἂν πείσαις ποτέ.   325

MH.   ἀλλ᾽ ἐξελᾷς με κοὐδὲν αἰδέσει λιτάς;

KP.   φιλῶ γὰρ οὐ σὲ μᾶλλον ἢ δόμους ἐμούς.

MH.   ὦ πατρίς, ὥς σου κάρτα νῦν μνείαν ἔχω.

KP.   πλὴν γὰρ τέκνων ἔμοιγε φίλτατον πολύ.

MH.   φεῦ φεῦ, βροτοῖς ἔρωτες ὡς κακὸν μέγα.   330

KP.   ὅπως ἄν, οἶμαι, καὶ παραστῶσιν τύχαι.

MH.   Ζεῦ, μὴ λάθοι σε τῶνδ᾽ ὃς αἴτιος κακῶν.

KP.   ἕρπ᾽ ὦ ματαία, καί μ᾽ ἀπάλλαξον πόνων.

MH.   πονοῦμεν ἡμεῖς κοὐ πόνων κεχρήμεθα.

KP.   τάχ᾽ ἐξ ὀπαδῶν χειρὸς ὠσθήσει βίᾳ.   335

MH.   μὴ δῆτα τοῦτό γ᾽, ἀλλά σ᾽ αἰτοῦμαι, Κρέον,

KP.   ὄχλον παρέξεις, ὡς ἔοικας, ὦ γύναι.

MH.   φευξούμεθ᾽· οὐ τοῦθ᾽ ἱκέτευσα σοῦ τυχεῖν.

KP.   τί οὖν βιάζει κοὐκ ἀπαλλάσσει χθονός;

MH.   μίαν με μεῖναι τήνδ᾽ ἔασον ἡμέραν   340
καὶ ξυμπερᾶναι φροντίδ᾽ ᾗ φευξούμεθα,
παισίν τ᾽ ἀφορμὴν τοῖς ἐμοῖς, ἐπεὶ πατὴρ
οὐδὲν προτιμᾷ μηχανήσασθαι τέκνοις.
οἴκτειρε δ᾽ αὐτούς· καὶ σύ τοι παίδων πατὴρ
πέφυκας· εἰκὸς δ᾽ ἐστὶν εὔνοιάν σ᾽ ἔχειν.   345
τοὐμοῦ γὰρ οὔ μοι φροντίς, εἰ φευξούμεθα,
κείνους δὲ κλαίω συμφορᾷ κεχρημένους.

KP.   ἥκιστα τοὐμὸν λῆμ᾽ ἔφυ τυραννικόν,
αἰδούμενος δὲ πολλὰ δὴ διέφθορα·
καὶ νῦν ὁρῶ μὲν ἐξαμαρτάνων, γύναι,   350
ὅμως δὲ τεύξει τοῦδε· προυννέπω δέ σοι,
εἴ σ᾽ ἡ ᾽πιοῦσα λαμπὰς ὄψεται θεοῦ
καὶ παῖδας ἐντὸς τῆσδε τερμόνων χθονός,
θανεῖ· λέλεκται μῦθος ἀψευδὴς ὅδε.
νῦν δ᾽, εἰ μένειν δεῖ, μίμν᾽ ἐφ᾽ ἡμέραν μίαν·   355
οὐ γάρ τι δράσεις δεινὸν ὧν φόβος μ᾽ ἔχει.

XO.   δύστανε γύναι,
φεῦ φεῦ, μελέα τῶν σῶν ἀχέων.

ποῖ ποτε τρέψει· τίνα προξενίαν
ἢ δόμον ἢ χθόνα σωτῆρα κακῶν;   360
ὡς εἰς ἄπορόν σε κλύδωνα θεός,
Μήδεια, κακῶν ἐπόρευσε.

ΜΗ. κακῶς πέπρακται πανταχῇ· τίς ἀντερεῖ;
ἀλλ' οὔτι ταύτῃ ταῦτα, μὴ δοκεῖτέ, πω.   365
ἔτ' εἴσ' ἀγῶνες τοῖς νεωστὶ νυμφίοις
καὶ τοῖσι κηδεύσασιν οὐ σμικροὶ πόνοι.
δοκεῖς γὰρ ἄν με τόνδε θωπεῦσαί ποτε,
εἰ μή τι κερδαίνουσαν ἢ τεχνωμένην;
οὐδ' ἂν προσεῖπον οὐδ' ἂν ἡψάμην χεροῖν.   370
ὁ δ' ἐς τοσοῦτον μωρίας ἀφίκετο,
ὥστ' ἐξὸν αὐτῷ τἄμ' ἑλεῖν βουλεύματα
γῆς ἐκβαλόντι, τήνδ' ἀφῆκεν ἡμέραν
μεῖναί μ', ἐν ᾗ τρεῖς τῶν ἐμῶν ἐχθρῶν νεκροὺς
θήσω, πατέρα τε καὶ κόρην πόσιν τ' ἐμόν.   375
πολλὰς δ' ἔχουσα θανασίμους αὐτοῖς ὁδούς,
οὐκ οἶδ' ὁποίᾳ πρῶτον ἐγχειρῶ, φίλαι,
πότερον ὑφάψω δῶμα νυμφικὸν πυρί,
ἢ θηκτὸν ὤσω φάσγανον δι' ἥπατος,
σιγῇ δόμους ἐσβᾶσ' ἵν' ἔστρωται λέχος.   380
ἀλλ' ἕν τί μοι πρόσαντες· εἰ ληφθήσομαι
δόμους ὑπερβαίνουσα καὶ τεχνωμένη,
θανοῦσα θήσω τοῖς ἐμοῖς ἐχθροῖς γέλων.
κράτιστα τὴν εὐθεῖαν, ᾗ πεφύκαμεν
σοφοὶ μάλιστα, φαρμάκοις αὐτοὺς ἑλεῖν.   385
εἶεν·
καὶ δὴ τεθνᾶσι· τίς με δέξεται πόλις;
τίς γῆν ἄσυλον καὶ δόμους ἐχεγγύους
ξένος παρασχὼν ῥύσεται τοὐμὸν δέμας;
οὐκ ἔστι. μείνασ' οὖν ἔτι σμικρὸν χρόνον,
ἢν μέν τις ἡμῖν πύργος ἀσφαλὴς φανῇ,   390
δόλῳ μέτειμι τόνδε καὶ σιγῇ φόνον·
ἢν δ' ἐξελαύνῃ συμφορά μ' ἀμήχανον,
αὐτὴ ξίφος λαβοῦσα, κεἰ μέλλω θανεῖν,
κτενῶ σφε, τόλμης δ' εἶμι πρὸς τὸ καρτερόν.
οὐ γὰρ μὰ τὴν δέσποιναν ἣν ἐγὼ σέβω   395
μάλιστα πάντων καὶ ξυνεργὸν εἱλόμην,
Ἑκάτην, μυχοῖς ναίουσαν ἑστίας ἐμῆς,
χαίρων τις αὐτῶν τοὐμὸν ἀλγυνεῖ κέαρ.
πικροὺς δ' ἐγώ σφιν καὶ λυγροὺς θήσω γάμους,
πικρὸν δὲ κῆδος καὶ φυγὰς ἐμὰς χθονός.   400
ἀλλ' εἶα· φείδου μηδὲν ὧν ἐπίστασαι,
Μήδεια, βουλεύουσα καὶ τεχνωμένη·
ἕρπ' ἐς τὸ δεινόν· νῦν ἀγὼν εὐψυχίας.
ὁρᾷς ἃ πάσχεις· οὐ γέλωτα δεῖ σ' ὀφλεῖν

τοῖς Σισυφείοις τοῖσδ' Ἰάσονος γάμοις,   405
γεγῶσαν ἐσθλοῦ πατρὸς Ἡλίου τ' ἄπο.
ἐπίστασαι δέ· πρὸς δὲ καὶ πεφύκαμεν
γυναῖκες, ἐς μὲν ἔσθλ' ἀμηχανώταται,
κακῶν δὲ πάντων τέκτονες σοφώταται.

XO. ἄνω ποταμῶν ἱερῶν χωροῦσι παγαί,   410
καὶ δίκα καὶ πάντα πάλιν στρέφεται.
ἀνδράσι μὲν δόλιαι βουλαί, θεῶν δ
οὐκέτι πίστις ἄραρε.
τὰν δ' ἐμὰν εὔκλειαν ἔχειν βιοτὰν   415
στρέψουσι φᾶμαι·
ἔρχεται τιμὰ γυναικείῳ γένει·
οὐκέτι δυσκέλαδος φάμα γυναῖκας ἕξει.   420
μοῦσαι δὲ παλαιγενέων λήξουσ' ἀοιδᾶν
τὰν ἐμὰν ὑμνεῦσαι ἀπιστοσύναν.
οὐ γὰρ ἐν ἀμετέρᾳ γνώμᾳ λύρας
ὤπασε θέσπιν ἀοιδὰν   425
Φοῖβος, ἡγήτωρ μελέων· ἐπεὶ ἀντ-
άχησ' ἂν ὕμνον
ἀρσένων γέννᾳ. μακρὸς δ' αἰὼν ἔχει
πολλὰ μὲν ἀμετέραν ἀνδρῶν τε μοῖραν εἰπεῖν.   430
σὺ δ' ἐκ μὲν οἴκων πατρίων ἔπλευσας
μαινομένᾳ κραδίᾳ, διδύμους ὁρίσασα πόντου
πέτρας, ἐπὶ δὲ ξένᾳ
ναίεις χθονί· τᾶς ἄνανδρος,   435
κοίτας ὀλέσασα λέκτρων,
τάλαινα, φυγάς τε χώρας
ἄτιμος ἐλαύνει.
βέβακε δ' ὅρκων χάρις, οὐδ' ἔτ' αἰδὼς
Ἑλλάδι τᾷ μεγάλᾳ μένει, αἰθερία δ' ἀνέπτα.   440
σοὶ δ' οὔτε πατρὸς δόμοι,
δύστανε, μεθορμίσασθαι
μόχθων πάρα, σῶν τε λέκτρων
ἄλλα βασίλεια κρείσσων
δόμοισιν ἐπέστα.   445

ΙΑΣΩΝ.

οὐ νῦν κατεῖδον πρῶτον ἀλλὰ πολλάκις
τραχεῖαν ὀργὴν ὡς ἀμήχανον κακόν.
σοὶ γὰρ παρὸν γῆν τήνδε καὶ δόμους ἔχειν
κούφως φερούσῃ κρεισσόνων βουλεύματα,
λόγων ματαίων εἵνεκ' ἐκπεσεῖ χθονός.   450
κἀμοὶ μὲν οὐδὲν πρᾶγμα· μὴ παύσῃ ποτὲ
λέγουσ' Ἰάσων ὡς κάκιστός ἐστ' ἀνήρ·
ἃ δ' ἐς τυράννους ἐστί σοι λελεγμένα,
πᾶν κέρδος ἡγοῦ ζημιουμένη φυγῇ.

κἀγὼ μὲν αἰεὶ βασιλέων θυμουμένων   455
ὀργὰς ἀφῄρουν καί σ' ἐβουλόμην μένειν·
σὺ δ' οὐκ ἀνίεις μωρίας, λέγουσ' ἀεὶ
κακῶς τυράννους· τοιγὰρ ἐκπεσεῖ χθονός.
ὅμως δὲ κἀκ τῶνδ' οὐκ ἀπειρηκὼς φίλοις
ἥκω, τόσον γε προσκοπούμενος, γύναι,   460
ὡς μήτ' ἀχρήμων σὺν τέκνοισιν ἐκπέσῃς
μήτ' ἐνδεής του· πόλλ' ἐφέλκεται φυγὴ
κακὰ ξὺν αὑτῇ. καὶ γὰρ εἰ σύ με στυγεῖς,
οὐκ ἂν δυναίμην σοὶ κακῶς φρονεῖν ποτε.
ΜΗ.   ὦ παγκάκιστε, τοῦτο γάρ σ' εἰπεῖν ἔχω,   465
γλώσσῃ μέγιστον εἰς ἀνανδρίαν κακόν,
ἦλθες πρὸς ἡμᾶς, ἦλθες ἔχθιστος γεγώς;
οὔτοι θράσος τόδ' ἐστὶν οὐδ' εὐτολμία,
φίλους κακῶς δράσαντ' ἐναντίον βλέπειν,   470
ἀλλ' ἡ μεγίστη τῶν ἐν ἀνθρώποις νόσων
πασῶν, ἀναίδει'· εὖ δ' ἐποίησας μολών·
ἐγώ τε γὰρ λέξασα κουφισθήσομαι
ψυχὴν κακῶς σε καὶ σὺ λυπήσει κλύων.
ἐκ τῶν δὲ πρώτων πρῶτον ἄρξομαι λέγειν.   475
ἔσωσά σ', ὡς ἴσασιν Ἑλλήνων ὅσοι
ταὐτὸν συνεισέβησαν Ἀργῷον σκάφος,
πεμφθέντα ταύρων πυρπνόων ἐπιστάτην
ζεύγλαισι καὶ σπεροῦντα θανάσιμον γύην·
δράκοντά θ', ὃς πάγχρυσον ἀμπέχων δέρας   480
σπείραις ἔσῳζε πολυπλόκοις ἄυπνος ὤν,
κτείνασ' ἀνέσχον σοὶ φάος σωτήριον.
αὐτὴ δὲ πατέρα καὶ δόμους προδοῦσ' ἐμοὺς
τὴν Πηλιῶτιν εἰς Ἰωλκὸν ἱκόμην
σὺν σοί, πρόθυμος μᾶλλον ἢ σοφωτέρα,   485
Πελίαν τ' ἀπέκτειν', ὥσπερ ἄλγιστον θανεῖν,
παίδων ὑπ' αὐτοῦ, πάντα δ' ἐξεῖλον φόβον.
καὶ ταῦθ' ὑφ' ἡμῶν, ὦ κάκιστ' ἀνδρῶν, παθὼν
προύδωκας ἡμᾶς, καινὰ δ' ἐκτήσω λέχη,
παίδων γεγώτων· εἰ γὰρ ἦσθ' ἄπαις ἔτι,   490
συγγνώστ' ἂν ἦν σοι τοῦδ' ἐρασθῆναι λέχους.
ὅρκων δὲ φρούδη πίστις, οὐδ' ἔχω μαθεῖν
εἰ θεοὺς νομίζεις τοὺς τότ' οὐκ ἄρχειν ἔτι,
ἢ καινὰ κεῖσθαι θέσμ' ἐν ἀνθρώποις τὰ νῦν,
ἐπεὶ σύνοισθά γ' εἰς ἔμ' οὐκ εὔορκος ὤν.   495
φεῦ δεξιὰ χείρ, ἧς σὺ πόλλ' ἐλαμβάνου,
καὶ τῶνδε γονάτων, ὡς μάτην κεχρώσμεθα
κακοῦ πρὸς ἀνδρός, ἐλπίδων δ' ἡμάρτομεν.
ἄγ'· ὡς φίλῳ γὰρ ὄντι σοι κοινώσομαι,
δοκοῦσα μὲν τί πρός γε σοῦ πράξειν καλῶς;   500
ὅμως δ'· ἐρωτηθεὶς γὰρ αἰσχίων φανεῖ.

νῦν ποῖ τράπωμαι; πότερα πρὸς πατρὸς δόμους,
οὓς σοὶ προδοῦσα καὶ πάτραν ἀφικόμην;
ἢ πρὸς ταλαίνας Πελιάδας; καλῶς γ' ἂν οὖν
δέξαιντό μ' οἴκοις ὧν πατέρα κατέκτανον.   505
ἔχει γὰρ οὕτω· τοῖς μὲν οἴκοθεν φίλοις
ἐχθρὰ καθέστηχ', οὓς δέ μ' οὐκ ἐχρῆν κακῶς
δρᾶν, σοὶ χάριν φέρουσα πολεμίους ἔχω.
τοιγάρ με πολλαῖς μακαρίαν Ἑλληνίδων
ἔθηκας ἀντὶ τῶνδε· θαυμαστὸν δέ σε   510
ἔχω πόσιν καὶ πιστὸν ἡ τάλαιν' ἐγώ,
εἰ φεύξομαί γε γαῖαν ἐκβεβλημένη,
φίλων ἔρημος, σὺν τέκνοις μόνη μόνοις,
καλόν γ' ὄνειδος τῷ νεωστὶ νυμφίῳ,
πτωχοὺς ἀλᾶσθαι παῖδας ἥ τ' ἔσωσά σε.   515
ὦ Ζεῦ, τί δὴ χρυσοῦ μὲν ὃς κίβδηλος ᾖ
τεκμήρι' ἀνθρώποισιν ὤπασας σαφῆ,
ἀνδρῶν δ' ὅτῳ χρὴ τὸν κακὸν διειδέναι,
οὐδεὶς χαρακτὴρ ἐμπέφυκε σώματι;
ΧΟ. δεινή τις ὀργὴ καὶ δυσίατος πέλει,   520
ὅταν φίλοι φίλοισι συμβάλωσ' ἔριν.
ΙΑ. δεῖ μ', ὡς ἔοικε, μὴ κακὸν φῦναι λέγειν,
ἀλλ' ὥστε ναὸς κεδνὸν οἰακοστρόφον
ἄκροισι λαίφους κρασπέδοις ὑπεκδραμεῖν
τὴν σὴν στόμαργον, ὦ γύναι, γλωσσαλγίαν.   525
ἐγὼ δ', ἐπειδὴ καὶ λίαν πυργοῖς χάριν,
Κύπριν νομίζω τῆς ἐμῆς ναυκληρίας
σώτειραν εἶναι θεῶν τε κἀνθρώπων μόνην.
σοὶ δ' ἔστι μὲν νοῦς λεπτός,—ἀλλ' ἐπίφθονος
λόγος διελθεῖν, ὡς Ἔρως σ' ἠνάγκασε   530
†τόξοις ἀφύκτοις τοὐμὸν ἐκσῶσαι δέμας.
ἀλλ' οὐκ ἀκριβῶς αὐτὸ θήσομαι λίαν·
ὅπῃ γὰρ οὖν ὤνησας, οὐ κακῶς ἔχει.
μείζω γε μέντοι τῆς ἐμῆς σωτηρίας
εἴληφας ἢ δέδωκας, ὡς ἐγὼ φράσω.   535
πρῶτον μὲν Ἑλλάδ' ἀντὶ βαρβάρου χθονὸς
γαῖαν κατοικεῖς καὶ δίκην ἐπίστασαι
νόμοις τε χρῆσθαι μὴ πρὸς ἰσχύος χάριν·
πάντες δέ σ' ᾔσθοντ' οὖσαν Ἕλληνες σοφὴν
καὶ δόξαν ἔσχες· εἰ δὲ γῆς ἐπ' ἐσχάτοις   540
ὅροισιν ᾤκεις, οὐκ ἂν ἦν λόγος σέθεν.
εἴη δ' ἔμοιγε μήτε χρυσὸς ἐν δόμοις
μήτ' Ὀρφέως κάλλιον ὑμνῆσαι μέλος,
εἰ μὴ 'πίσημος ἡ τύχη γένοιτό μοι.
τοσαῦτα μέν σοι τῶν ἐμῶν πόνων πέρι   545
ἔλεξ'· ἅμιλλαν γὰρ σὺ προύθηκας λόγων.
ἃ δ' ἐς γάμους μοι βασιλικοὺς ὠνείδισας,

ἐν τῷδε δείξω πρῶτα μὲν σοφὸς γεγώς,
ἔπειτα σώφρων, εἶτα σοὶ μέγας φίλος
καὶ παισὶ τοῖς ἐμοῖσιν· ἀλλ' ἔχ' ἥσυχος.　　　550
ἐπεὶ μετέστην δεῦρ' Ἰωλκίας χθονὸς
πολλὰς ἐφέλκων συμφορὰς ἀμηχάνους,
τί τοῦδ' ἂν εὕρημ' ηὗρον εὐτυχέστερον
ἢ παῖδα γῆμαι βασιλέως φυγὰς γεγώς;
οὐχ, ᾗ σὺ κνίζει, σὸν μὲν ἐχθαίρων λέχος,　　　555
καινῆς δὲ νύμφης ἱμέρῳ πεπληγμένος,
οὐδ' εἰς ἅμιλλαν πολύτεκνον σπουδὴν ἔχων·
ἅλις γὰρ οἱ γεγῶτες οὐδὲ μέμφομαι·
ἀλλ' ὡς τὸ μὲν μέγιστον οἰκοῖμεν καλῶς
καὶ μὴ σπανιζοίμεσθα, γιγνώσκων ὅτι　　　560
πένητα φεύγει πᾶς τις ἐκποδὼν φίλος,
παῖδας δὲ θρέψαιμ' ἀξίως δόμων ἐμῶν
σπείρας τ' ἀδελφοὺς τοῖσιν ἐκ σέθεν τέκνοις
ἐς ταὐτὸ θείην καὶ ξυναρτήσας γένος
εὐδαιμονοῖμεν. σοί τε γὰρ παίδων τί δεῖ;　　　565
ἐμοί τε λύει τοῖσι μέλλουσιν τέκνοις
τὰ ζῶντ' ὀνῆσαι. μῶν βεβούλευμαι κακῶς;
οὐδ' ἂν σὺ φαίης, εἴ σε μὴ κνίζοι λέχος.
ἀλλ' ἐς τοσοῦτον ἥκεθ' ὥστ' ὀρθουμένης
εὐνῆς γυναῖκες πάντ' ἔχειν νομίζετε,　　　570
ἢν δ' αὖ γένηται ξυμφορά τις ἐς λέχος,
τὰ λῷστα καὶ κάλλιστα πολεμιώτατα
τίθεσθε. χρῆν γὰρ ἄλλοθέν ποθεν βροτοὺς
παῖδας τεκνοῦσθαι, θῆλυ δ' οὐκ εἶναι γένος·
χοὕτως ἂν οὐκ ἦν οὐδὲν ἀνθρώποις κακόν.　　　575
ΧΟ. Ἰᾶσον, εὖ μὲν τούσδ' ἐκόσμησας λόγους·
ὅμως δ' ἔμοιγε, κεἰ παρὰ γνώμην ἐρῶ,
δοκεῖς προδοὺς σὴν ἄλοχον οὐ δίκαια δρᾶν.
ΜΗ. ἦ πολλὰ πολλοῖς εἰμι διάφορος βροτῶν.
ἐμοὶ γὰρ ὅστις ἄδικος ὢν σοφὸς λέγειν　　　580
πέφυκε, πλείστην ζημίαν ὀφλισκάνει·
γλώσσῃ γὰρ αὐχῶν τἄδικ' εὖ περιστελεῖν,
τολμᾷ πανουργεῖν· ἔστι δ' οὐκ ἄγαν σοφός.
ὡς καὶ σύ· μή νυν εἰς ἔμ' εὐσχήμων γένῃ
λέγειν τε δεινός. ἐν γὰρ ἐκτενεῖ σ' ἔπος·　　　585
χρῆν σ', εἴπερ ἦσθα μὴ κακός, πείσαντά με
γαμεῖν γάμον τόνδ', ἀλλὰ μὴ σιγῇ φίλων.
ΙΑ. καλῶς γ' ἄν, οἶμαι, τῷδ' ὑπηρέτεις λόγῳ,
εἴ σοι γάμον κατεῖπον, ἥτις οὐδὲ νῦν
τολμᾷς μεθεῖναι καρδίας μέγαν χόλον.　　　590
ΜΗ. οὐ τοῦτό σ' εἶχεν, ἀλλὰ βάρβαρον λέχος
πρὸς γῆρας οὐκ εὔδοξον ἐξέβαινέ σοι.
ΙΑ. εὖ νῦν τόδ' ἴσθι, μὴ γυναικὸς εἵνεκα

γῆμαί με λέκτρα βασιλέων ἃ νῦν ἔχω,
ἀλλ᾽, ὥσπερ εἶπον καὶ πάρος; σῶσαι θέλων 595
σὲ καὶ τέκνοισι τοῖς ἐμοῖς ὁμοσπόρους
φῦσαι τυράννους παῖδας, ἔρυμα δώμασι.

MH. μή μοι γένοιτο λυπρὸς εὐδαίμων βίος
μηδ᾽ ὄλβος ὅστις τὴν ἐμὴν κνίζοι φρένα.

IA. οἶσθ᾽ ὡς μέτευξαι καὶ σοφωτέρα φανεῖ; 600
τὰ χρηστὰ μή σοι λυπρὰ φαινέσθω ποτέ,
μηδ᾽ εὐτυχοῦσα δυστυχὴς εἶναι δόκει.

MH. ὕβριζ᾽, ἐπειδὴ σοὶ μὲν ἔστ᾽ ἀποστροφή,
ἐγὼ δ᾽ ἔρημος τήνδε φευξοῦμαι χθόνα.

IA. αὐτὴ τάδ᾽ εἵλου· μηδέν᾽ ἄλλον αἰτιῶ. 605

MH. τί δρῶσα; μῶν γαμοῦσα καὶ προδοῦσά σε;

IA. ἀρὰς τυράννοις ἀνοσίους ἀρωμένη.

MH. καὶ σοῖς ἀραία γ᾽ οὖσα τυγχάνω δόμοις.

IA. ὡς οὐ κρινοῦμαι τῶνδέ σοι τὰ πλείονα.
ἀλλ᾽, εἴ τι βούλει παισὶν ἢ σαυτῆς φυγῇ 610
προσωφέλημα χρημάτων ἐμῶν λαβεῖν,
λέγ᾽· ὡς ἕτοιμος ἀφθόνῳ δοῦναι χερὶ
ξένοις τε πέμπειν σύμβολ᾽, οἳ δράσουσί σ᾽ εὖ.
καὶ ταῦτα μὴ θέλουσα μωρανεῖς, γύναι·
λήξασά δ᾽ ὀργῆς κερδανεῖς ἀμείνονα. 615

MH. οὔτ᾽ ἂν ξένοισι τοῖσι σοῖς χρησαίμεθ᾽ ἄν,
οὔτ᾽ ἄν τι δεξαίμεσθα, μήθ᾽ ἡμῖν δίδου·
κακοῦ γὰρ ἀνδρὸς δῶρ᾽ ὄνησιν οὐκ ἔχει.

IA. ἀλλ᾽ οὖν ἐγὼ μὲν δαίμονας μαρτύρομαι,
ὡς πάνθ᾽ ὑπουργεῖν σοί τε καὶ τέκνοις θέλω· 620
σοὶ δ᾽ οὐκ ἀρέσκει τἀγάθ᾽, ἀλλ᾽ αὐθαδίᾳ
φίλους ἀπωθεῖ· τοιγὰρ ἀλγυνεῖ πλέον.

MH. χώρει· πόθῳ γὰρ τῆς νεοδμήτου κόρης
αἱρεῖ χρονίζων δωμάτων ἐξώπιος.
νύμφευ᾽· ἴσως γάρ—σὺν θεῷ δ᾽ εἰρήσεται— 625
γαμεῖς τοιοῦτον ὥστε σ᾽ ἀρνεῖσθαι γάμον.

XO. ἔρωτες ὑπὲρ μὲν ἄγαν
ἐλθόντες οὐκ εὐδοξίαν
οὐδ᾽ ἀρετὰν παρέδωκαν
ἀνδράσιν· εἰ δ᾽ ἅλις ἔλθοι 630
Κύπρις, οὐκ ἄλλα θεὸς εὔχαρις οὕτως.
μήποτ᾽, ὦ δέσποιν᾽, ἐπ᾽ ἐμοὶ
χρυσέων τόξων ἐφείης
ἱμέρῳ χρίσασ᾽ ἄφυκτον οἰστόν.
στέργοι δέ με σωφροσύνα, 635
δώρημα κάλλιστον θεῶν·
μηδέ ποτ᾽ ἀμφιλόγους ὀρ-
γὰς ἀκόρεστά τε νείκη
θυμὸν ἐκπλήξασ᾽ ἑτέροις ἐπὶ λέκτροις

προσβάλοι δεινὰ Κύπρις, ἀ-   640
πτολέμους δ᾽ εὐνὰς σεβίζουσ᾽
ὀξύφρων κρίνοι λέχη γυναικῶν.
ὦ πατρίς, ὦ δώματα, μὴ
δῆτ᾽ ἄπολις γενοίμαν
τὸν ἀμηχανίας ἔχουσα   645
δυσπέρατον αἰῶν᾽,
οἰκτρότατον ἀχέων.
θανάτῳ θανάτῳ πάρος δαμείην
ἀμέραν τάνδ᾽ ἐξανύσασα· μό-
χθων δ᾽ οὐκ ἄλλος ὕπερθεν ἢ   650
γᾶς πατρίας στέρεσθαι.
εἴδομεν, οὐκ ἐξ ἑτέρων
μῦθον ἔχω φράσασθαι·
σὲ γὰρ οὐ πόλις, οὐ φίλων τις   655
ᾤκτειρεν παθοῦσαν
δεινότατα παθέων.
ἀχάριστος ὄλοιθ᾽, ὅτῳ πάρεστιν
μὴ φίλους τιμᾶν καθαρὰν ἀνοί-   660
ξαντα κλῇδα φρενῶν· ἐμοὶ
μὲν φίλος οὔποτ᾽ ἔσται.

ΑΙΓΕΥΣ.

Μήδεια, χαῖρε· τοῦδε γὰρ προοίμιον
κάλλιον οὐδεὶς οἶδε προσφωνεῖν φίλους.

MH.   ὦ χαῖρε καὶ σύ, παῖ σοφοῦ Πανδίονος,   665
    Αἰγεῦ. πόθεν γῆς τῆσδ᾽ ἐπιστρωφᾷ πέδον;
AI.   Φοίβου παλαιὸν ἐκλιπὼν χρηστήριον.
MH   τί δ᾽ ὀμφαλὸν γῆς θεσπιῳδὸν ἵζάνεις;
AI.   παίδων ἐρευνῶν σπέρμ᾽ ὅπως γένοιτό μοι.
MH.   πρὸς θεῶν, ἄπαις γὰρ δεῦρ᾽ ἀεὶ τείνεις βίον;   670
AI.   ἄπαιδές ἐσμεν δαίμονός τινος τύχῃ.
MH.   δάμαρτος οὔσης, ἢ λέχους ἄπειρος ὤν;
AI.   οὐκ ἐσμὲν εὐνῆς ἄζυγες γαμηλίου.
MH.   τί δῆτα Φοῖβος εἶπέ σοι παίδων πέρι;
AI.   σοφώτερ᾽ ἢ κατ᾽ ἄνδρα συμβαλεῖν ἔπη.   675
MH.   θέμις μὲν ἡμᾶς χρησμὸν εἰδέναι θεοῦ;
AI.   μάλιστ᾽, ἐπεί τοι καὶ σοφῆς δεῖται φρενός.
MH.   τί δῆτ᾽ ἔχρησε; λέξον, εἰ θέμις κλύειν.
AI.   ἀσκοῦ με τὸν προύχοντα μὴ λῦσαι πόδα,
MH.   πρὶν ἂν τί δράσῃς ἢ τίν᾽ ἐξίκῃ χθόνα;   680
AI.   πρὶν ἂν πατρῴαν αὖθις ἑστίαν μόλω.
MH.   σὺ δ᾽ ὡς τί χρῄζων τήνδε ναυστολεῖς χθόνα;
AI.   Πιτθεύς τις ἔστι, γῆς ἄναξ Τροιζηνίας.
MH.   παῖς, ὡς λέγουσι, Πέλοπος εὐσεβέστατος.
AI.   τούτῳ θεοῦ μάντευμα κοινῶσαι θέλω.   685

ΜΗ. σοφὸς γὰρ ἀνὴρ καὶ τρίβων τὰ τοιάδε.

ΑΙ. κἀμοί γε πάντων φίλτατος δορυξένων.

ΜΗ. ἀλλ' εὐτυχοίης καὶ τύχοις ὅσων ἐρᾷς.

ΑΙ. τί γὰρ σὸν ὄμμα χρώς τε συντέτηχ' ὅδε;

ΜΗ. Αἰγεῦ, κάκιστός ἐστί μοι πάντων πόσις. 690

ΑΙ. τί φής; σαφῶς μοι σὰς φράσον δυσθυμίας.

ΜΗ. ἀδικεῖ μ' Ἰάσων οὐδὲν ἐξ ἐμοῦ παθών.

ΑΙ. τί χρῆμα δράσας; φράζε μοι σαφέστερον.

ΜΗ. γυναῖκ' ἐφ' ἡμῖν δεσπότιν δόμων ἔχει.

ΑΙ. μή που τετόλμηκ' ἔργον αἴσχιστον τόδε; 695

ΜΗ. σάφ' ἴσθ'· ἄτιμοι δ' ἐσμὲν οἱ πρὸ τοῦ φίλοι.

ΑΙ. πότερον ἐρασθεὶς ἢ σὸν ἐχθαίρων λέχος;

ΜΗ. μέγαν γ' ἔρωτα πιστὸς οὐκ ἔφυ φίλοις.

ΑΙ. ἴτω νυν, εἴπερ, ὡς λέγεις, ἐστὶν κακός,—

ΜΗ. ἀνδρῶν τυράννων κῆδος ἠράσθη λαβεῖν. 700

ΑΙ. δίδωσι δ' αὐτῷ τίς; πέραινέ μοι λόγον.

ΜΗ. Κρέων, ὃς ἄρχει τῆσδε γῆς Κορινθίας.

ΑΙ. συγγνωστὰ γὰρ ἦν σε λυπεῖσθαι, γύναι.†

ΜΗ. ὄλωλα· καὶ πρός γ' ἐξελαύνομαι χθονός.

ΑΙ. πρὸς τοῦ; τόδ' ἄλλο καινὸν αὖ λέγεις κακόν. 705

ΜΗ. Κρέων μ' ἐλαύνει φυγάδα γῆς Κορινθίας.

ΑΙ. ἐᾷ δ' Ἰάσων; οὐδὲ ταῦτ' ἐπήνεσα.

ΜΗ. λόγῳ μὲν οὐχί, καρτερεῖν δὲ βούλεται.
   ἀλλ' ἄντομαί σε τῆσδε πρὸς γενειάδος
   γονάτων τε τῶν σῶν ἱκεσία τε γίγνομαι, 710
   οἴκτειρον οἴκτειρόν με τὴν δυσδαίμονα
   καὶ μή μ' ἔρημον ἐκπεσοῦσαν εἰσίδῃς,
   δέξαι δὲ χώρᾳ καὶ δόμοις ἐφέστιον.
   οὕτως ἔρως σοὶ πρὸς θεῶν τελεσφόρος
   γένοιτο παίδων, καὐτὸς ὄλβιος θάνοις. 715
   εὕρημα δ' οὐκ οἶσθ' οἷον ηὕρηκας τόδε·
   παύσω δέ σ' ὄντ' ἄπαιδα καὶ παίδων γονὰς
   σπεῖραί σε θήσω· τοιάδ' οἶδα φάρμακα.

ΑΙ. πολλῶν ἔκατι τήνδε σοι δοῦναι χάριν,
   γύναι, πρόθυμός εἰμι, πρᾶτα μὲν θεῶν, 720
   ἔπειτα παίδων ὧν ἐπαγγέλλει γονάς·
   ἐς τοῦτο γὰρ δὴ φροῦδός εἰμι πᾶς ἐγώ.
   οὕτω δ' ἔχει μοι· σοῦ μὲν ἐλθούσης χθόνα,
   πειράσομαί σου προξενεῖν δίκαιος ὤν.
   τοσόνδε μέντοι σοι προσημαίνω, γύναι· 725
   ἐκ τῆσδε μὲν γῆς οὔ σ' ἄγειν βουλήσομαι,
   αὐτὴ δ' ἐάνπερ εἰς ἐμοὺς ἔλθῃς δόμους,
   μενεῖς ἄσυλος κοὔ σε μὴ μεθῶ τινι.
   ἐκ τῆσδε δ' αὐτὴ γῆς ἀπαλλάσσου πόδα·
   ἀναίτιος γὰρ καὶ ξένοις εἶναι θέλω. 730

ΜΗ. ἔσται τάδ'· ἀλλὰ πίστις εἰ γένοιτό μοι

τούτων, ἔχοιμ' ἂν πάντα πρὸς σέθεν καλῶς.
ΑΙ.	μῶν οὐ πέποιθας; ἢ τί σοι τὸ δυσχερές;
ΜΗ.	πέποιθα· Πελίου δ' ἐχθρός ἐστί μοι δόμος
	Κρέων τε. τούτοις δ' ὁρκίοισι μὲν ζυγεὶς	735
	ἄγουσιν οὐ μεθεῖ' ἂν ἐκ γαίας ἐμέ·
	λόγοις δὲ συμβὰς καὶ θεῶν ἀνώμοτος
	ψιλὸς γένοι' ἂν κἀπικηρυκεύματα
	οὐκ ἀντισοῖο· τἀμὰ μὲν γὰρ ἀσθενῆ,·
	τοῖς δ' ὄλβος ἐστὶ καὶ δόμος τυραννικός.	740
ΑΙ.	πολλὴν ἔλεξας ἐν λόγοις προμηθίαν·
	ἀλλ', εἰ δοκεῖ σοι, δρᾶν τάδ' οὐκ ἀφίσταμαι.
	ἐμοί τε γὰρ τάδ' ἐστὶν ἀσφαλέστατα,
	σκῆψίν τιν' ἐχθροῖς σοῖς ἔχοντα δεικνύναι,
	τὸ σόν τ' ἄραρε μᾶλλον· ἐξηγοῦ θεούς.	745
ΜΗ.	ὄμνυ πέδον Γῆς πατέρα θ' Ἥλιον πατρὸς
	τοὐμοῦ θεῶν τε συντιθεὶς ἅπαν γένος.
ΑΙ.	τί χρῆμα δράσειν ἢ τί μὴ δράσειν; λέγε.
ΜΗ.	μήτ' αὐτὸς ἐκ γῆς σῆς ἔμ' ἐκβαλεῖν ποτε,
	μήτ' ἄλλος ἤν τις τῶν ἐμῶν ἐχθρῶν ἄγειν	750
	χρῄζῃ, μεθήσειν ζῶν ἑκουσίῳ τρόπῳ.
ΑΙ.	ὄμνυμι Γαίας δάπεδον Ἡλίου τε φῶς
	θεούς τε πάντας ἐμμενεῖν ἅ σου κλύω.
ΜΗ.	ἀρκεῖ· τί δ' ὅρκῳ τῷδε μὴ 'μμένων πάθοις;
ΑΙ.	ἃ τοῖσι δυσσεβοῦσι γίγνεται βροτῶν.	755
ΜΗ.	χαίρων πορεύου· πάντα γὰρ καλῶς ἔχει.
	κἀγὼ πόλιν σὴν ὡς τάχιστ' ἀφίξομαι,
	πράξασ' ἃ μέλλω καὶ τυχοῦσ' ἃ βούλομαι.
ΧΟ.	ἀλλά σ' ὁ Μαίας πομπαῖος ἄναξ
	πελάσειε δόμοις, ὧν τ' ἐπίνοιαν	760
	σπεύδεις κατέχων πράξειας, ἐπεὶ
	γενναῖος ἀνήρ,
	Αἰγεῦ, παρ' ἐμοὶ δεδόκησαι.
ΜΗ.	ὦ Ζεῦ Δίκη τε Ζηνὸς Ἡλίου τε φῶς,
	νῦν καλλίνικοι τῶν ἐμῶν ἐχθρῶν, φίλαι,	765
	γενησόμεσθα κεἰς ὁδὸν βεβήκαμεν·
	νῦν δ' ἐλπὶς ἐχθροὺς τοὺς ἐμοὺς τίσειν δίκην.
	οὗτος γὰρ ἀνὴρ ᾗ μάλιστ' ἐκάμνομεν
	λιμὴν πέφανται τῶν ἐμῶν βουλευμάτων·
	ἐκ τοῦδ' ἀναψόμεσθα πρυμνήτην κάλων,	770
	μολόντες ἄστυ καὶ πόλισμα Παλλάδος.
	ἤδη δὲ πάντα τἀμά σοι βουλεύματα
	λέξω· δέχου δὲ μὴ πρὸς ἡδονὴν λόγους.
	πέμψασ' ἐμῶν τιν' οἰκετῶν Ἰάσονα
	ἐς ὄψιν ἐλθεῖν τὴν ἐμὴν αἰτήσομαι·	775
	μολόντι δ' αὐτῷ μαλθακοὺς λέξω λόγους,
	ὡς καὶ δοκεῖ μοι ταῦτα καὶ καλῶς ἔχει,

γάμους τυράννων οὓς προδοὺς ἡμᾶς ἔχει
καὶ ξύμφορ' εἶναι καὶ καλῶς ἐγνωσμένα·
παῖδας δὲ μεῖναι τοὺς ἐμοὺς αἰτήσομαι,   780
οὐχ ὡς λιποῦσ' ἂν πολεμίας ἐπὶ χθονός,
ἐχθροῖσι παῖδας τοὺς ἐμοὺς καθυβρίσαι,
ἀλλ' ὡς δόλοισι παῖδα βασιλέως κτάνω.
πέμψω γὰρ αὐτοὺς δῶρ' ἔχοντας ἐν χεροῖν
νύμφῃ φέροντας δῆθεν μὴ φεύγειν χθόνα,   785
λεπτόν τε πέπλον καὶ πλόκον χρυσήλατον·
κἄνπερ λαβοῦσα κόσμον ἀμφιθῇ χροΐ,
κακῶς ὀλεῖται πᾶς θ' ὃς ἂν θίγῃ κόρης·
τοιοῖσδε χρίσω φαρμάκοις δωρήματα.
ἐνταῦθα μέντοι τόνδ' ἀπαλλάσσω λόγον·   790
ᾤμωξα δ' οἷον ἔργον ἔστ' ἐργαστέον
τοὐντεῦθεν ἡμῖν· τέκνα γὰρ κατακτενῶ
τἄμ'· οὔτις ἔστιν ὅστις ἐξαιρήσεται·
δόμον τε πάντα συγχέασ' Ἰάσονος
ἔξειμι γαίας, φιλτάτων παίδων φόνον   795
φεύγουσα καὶ τλᾶσ' ἔργον ἀνοσιώτατον.
οὐ γὰρ γελᾶσθαι τλητὸν ἐξ ἐχθρῶν, φίλαι.
ἴτω· τί μοι ζῆν κέρδος; οὔτε μοι πατρὶς
οὔτ' οἶκος ἔστιν οὔτ' ἀποστροφὴ κακῶν.
ἡμάρτανον τόθ' ἡνίκ' ἐξελίμπανον   800
δόμους πατρῴους, ἀνδρὸς Ἕλληνος λόγοις
πεισθεῖσ', ὃς ἡμῖν σὺν θεῷ τίσει δίκην.
οὔτ' ἐξ ἐμοῦ γὰρ παῖδας ὄψεταί ποτε
ζῶντας τὸ λοιπὸν οὔτε τῆς νεοζύγου
νύμφης τεκνώσει παῖδ', ἐπεὶ κακὴν κακῶς   805
θανεῖν σφ' ἀνάγκη τοῖς ἐμοῖσι φαρμάκοις.
μηδείς με φαύλην κἀσθενῆ νομιζέτω
μηδ' ἡσυχαίαν, ἀλλὰ θατέρου τρόπου,
βαρεῖαν ἐχθροῖς καὶ φίλοισιν εὐμενῆ·
τῶν γὰρ τοιούτων εὐκλεέστατος βίος.   810

ΧΟ. ἐπείπερ ἡμῖν τόνδ' ἐκοίνωσας λόγον,
σέ τ' ὠφελεῖν θέλουσα καὶ νόμοις βροτῶν
ξυλλαμβάνουσα δρᾶν σ' ἀπεννέπω τάδε.

ΜΗ. οὐκ ἔστιν ἄλλως· σοὶ δὲ συγγνώμη λέγειν
τάδ' ἐστί, μὴ πάσχουσαν, ὡς ἐγώ, κακῶς.   815

ΧΟ. ἀλλὰ κτανεῖν σὸν σπέρμα τολμήσεις, γύναι;

ΜΗ. οὕτω γὰρ ἂν μάλιστα δηχθείη πόσις.

ΧΟ. σὺ δ' ἂν γένοιό γ' ἀθλιωτάτη γυνή.

ΜΗ. ἴτω· περισσοὶ πάντες οὑν μέσῳ λόγοι.
ἀλλ' εἶα χώρει καὶ κόμιζ' Ἰάσονα·   820
ἐς πάντα γὰρ δὴ σοὶ τὰ πιστὰ χρώμεθα.
λέξῃς δὲ μηδὲν τῶν ἐμοὶ δεδογμένων,

εἴπερ φρονεῖς εὖ δεσπόταις γυνή τ' ἔφυς.

XO Ἐρεχθεῖδαι τὸ παλαιὸν ὄλβιοι
καὶ θεῶν παῖδες μακάρων ἱερᾶς 825
χώρας ἀπορθήτου τ' ἄπο,—φερβόμενοι
κλεινοτάταν σοφίαν, αἰεὶ διὰ λαμπροτάτου
βαίνοντες ἁβρῶς αἰθέρος, ἔνθα ποθ' ἁγνὰς 830
ἐννέα Πιερίδας Μούσας λέγουσι
ξανθὰν Ἁρμονίαν φυτεῦσαι—
τοῦ καλλινάου τ' ἀπὸ Κηφισοῦ ῥοᾶς, ἀντ. 835
τὰν Κύπριν κλῄζουσιν ἀφυσσομέναν
χώραν καταπλεῦσαι μετρίοις ἀνέμων
ἡδυπνόοις αὔραις, αἰεὶ δ' ἐπιβαλλομέναν 840
χαίταισιν εὐώδη ῥοδέων πλόκον ἀνθέων
τᾷ σοφίᾳ παρέδρους πέμπειν ἔρωτας,
παντοίας ἀρετᾶς ξυνεργούς. 845
πῶς οὖν ἱερῷ ποταμῷ στρ.
ἢ φίλῳ ἢ πόλις
πόμπιμός σε χώρᾳ
τὰν παιδολέτειραν ἕξει,
τὰν οὐχ ὁσίαν, μεταλλῶ. 850
σκέψαι τεκέων πλαγάν.
σκέψαι φόνον οἷον αἴρει.
μή, πρὸς γονάτων σε πάντως
πάντη θ' ἱκετεύομεν,
τέκνα φονεύσῃς. 855
πόθεν θράσος ἢ φρενὸς ἢ ἀντ.
χειρὶ σέθεν τέχναν
καρδίᾳ τε λήψει
δεινὰν προσάγουσα τόλμαν;
πῶς δ' ὄμματα προσβαλοῦσα 860
τέκνοις ἄδακρυν μοῖραν
σχήσεις φόνου; οὐ δυνάσει,
παίδων ἱκετᾶν πιτνόντων,
τέγξαι χέρα φοινίαν
τλάμονι θυμῷ. 865

ΙΑ. ἥκω κελευσθείς· καὶ γὰρ οὖσα δυσμενὴς
οὔ τἂν ἁμάρτοις τοῦδέ γ', ἀλλ' ἀκούσομαι
τί χρῆμα βούλει καινὸν ἐξ ἐμοῦ, γύναι.

ΜΗ. Ἰᾶσον, αἰτοῦμαί σε τῶν εἰρημένων
συγγνώμον' εἶναι· τὰς δ' ἐμὰς ὀργὰς φέρειν 870
εἰκός σ', ἐπεὶ νῷν πόλλ' ὑπείργασται φίλα.
ἐγὼ δ' ἐμαυτῇ διὰ λόγων ἀφικόμην
κἀλοιδόρησα· σχετλία, τί μαίνομαι
καὶ δυσμεναίνω τοῖσι βουλεύουσιν εὖ,
ἐχθρὰ δὲ γαίας κοιράνοις καθίσταμαι 875

πόσει θ', ὃς ἡμῖν δρᾷ τὰ συμφορώτατα,
γήμας τύραννον καὶ κασιγνήτους τέκνοις
ἐμοῖς φυτεύων; οὐκ ἀπαλλαχθήσομαι
θυμοῦ; τί πάσχω, θεῶν πορthat ζόντων καλῶς;
οὐκ εἰσὶ μέν μοι παῖδες, οἶδα δὲ χθόνα   880
φεύγοντας ἡμᾶς καὶ σπανίζοντας φίλων;
ταῦτ' ἐννοηθεῖσ' ᾐσθόμην ἀβουλίαν
πολλὴν ἔχουσα καὶ μάτην θυμουμένη.
νῦν οὖν ἐπαινῶ σωφρονεῖν τέ μοι δοκεῖς
κῆδος τόδ' ἡμῖν προσλαβών, ἐγὼ δ' ἄφρων,   885
ᾗ χρῆν μετεῖναι τῶνδε τῶν βουλευμάτων
καὶ ξυνυμεναιεῖν καὶ παρεστάναι λέχει
νύμφῃ τε κηδεύουσαν ἥδεσθαι σέθεν.
ἀλλ' ἐσμὲν οἷόν ἐσμεν, οὐκ ἐρῶ κακόν,
γυναῖκες· οὔκουν χρὴ 'ξομοιοῦσθαι κακοῖς   890
οὐδ' ἀντιτείνειν, νήπι' ἀντὶ νηπίων.
παριέμεσθα, καί φαμεν κακῶς φρονεῖν
τότ', ἀλλ' ἄμεινον νῦν βεβούλευμαι τόδε·
ὦ τέκνα τέκνα, δεῦτε, λείπετε στέγας,
ἐξέλθετ', ἀσπάσασθε καὶ προσείπατε   895
πατέρα μεθ' ἡμῶν, καὶ διαλλάχθηθ' ἅμα
τῆς πρόσθεν ἔχθρας ἐς φίλους μητρὸς μέτα·
σπονδαὶ γὰρ ἡμῖν καὶ μεθέστηκεν χόλος.
λάβεσθε χειρὸς δεξιᾶς. οἴμοι, κακῶν
ὡς ἐννοοῦμαι δή τι τῶν κεκρυμμένων.   900
ἆρ', ὦ τέκν', οὕτω καὶ πολὺν ζῶντες χρόνον
φίλην ὀρέξετ' ὠλένην; τάλαιν' ἐγώ,
ὡς ἀρτίδακρύς εἰμι καὶ φόβου πλέα.
χρόνῳ δὲ νεῖκος πατρὸς ἐξαιρουμένη
ὄψιν τέρειναν τήνδ' ἔπλησα δακρύων.   905
ΧΟ.   κἀμοὶ κατ' ὄσσων χλωρὸν ὡρμήθη δάκρυ·
καὶ μὴ προβαίη μᾶσσον ἢ τὸ νῦν κακόν.
ΙΑ.   αἰνῶ, γύναι, τάδ', οὐδ' ἐκεῖνα μέμφομαι.
εἰκὸς γὰρ ὀργὰς θῆλυ ποιεῖσθαι γένος
γάμους παρεμπολῶντι συλαίους πόσει.   910
ἀλλ' ἐς τὸ λῷον σὸν μεθέστηκεν κέαρ,
ἔγνως δὲ τὴν νικῶσαν ἀλλὰ τῷ χρόνῳ.
βουλήν· γυναικὸς ἔργα ταῦτα σώφρονος.
ὑμῖν δέ, παῖδες, οὐκ ἀφρόντιστος πατὴρ
πολλὴ δ' ἔθ' ἥξει σὺν θεοῖς σωτηρία.*   915
οἶμαι γὰρ ὑμᾶς τῆσδε γῆς Κορινθίας
τὰ πρῶτ' ἔσεσθαι σὺν κασιγνήτοις ἔτι.
ἀλλ' αὐξάνεσθε· τἄλλα δ' ἐξεργάζεται
πατήρ τε καὶ θεῶν ὅστις ἐστὶν εὐμενής·
ἴδοιμι δ' ὑμᾶς εὐτραφεῖς ἥβης τέλος   920
μολόντας, ἐχθρῶν τῶν ἐμῶν ὑπερτέρους.

αὕτη, τί χλωροῖς δακρύοις τέγγεις κόρας,
στρέψασα λευκὴν ἔμπαλιν παρηίδα,
κοὐκ ἀσμένη τόνδ' ἐξ ἐμοῦ δέχει λόγον;
MH. οὐδέν. τέκνων τῶνδ' ἐννοουμένη πέρι.   925
IA. θάρσει νυν· εὖ γὰρ τῶνδ' ἐγὼ θήσω πέρι.
MH. δράσω τάδ'· οὔτοι σοῖς ἀπιστήσω λόγοις.
γυνὴ δὲ θῆλυ κἀπὶ δακρύοις ἔφυ.
IA. τί δῆτα λίαν τοῖσδ' ἐπιστένεις τέκνοις;
MH. ἔτικτον αὐτούς· ζῆν δ' ὅτ' ἐξηύχου τέκνα,   930
ἐσῆλθέ μ' οἶκτος εἰ γενήσεται τάδε.
ἀλλ' ὧνπερ εἵνεκ' εἰς ἐμοὺς ἥκεις λόγους,
τὰ μὲν λέλεκται, τῶν δ' ἐγὼ μνησθήσομαι.
ἐπεὶ τυράννοις γῆς μ' ἀποστεῖλαι δοκεῖ,
κἀμοὶ τάδ' ἐστὶ λῷστα, γιγνώσκω καλῶς,   935
μήτ' ἐμποδὼν σοὶ μήτε κοιράνοις χθονὸς
ναίειν—δοκῶ γὰρ δυσμενὴς εἶναι δόμοις—
ἡμεῖς μὲν ἐκ γῆς τῆσδ' ἀπαίρομεν φυγῇ,
παῖδας δ' ὅπως ἂν ἐκτραφῶσι σῇ χερί
αἰτοῦ Κρέοντα τήνδε μὴ φεύγειν χθόνα.   940
IA. οὐκ οἶδ' ἂν εἰ πείσαιμι, πειρᾶσθαι δὲ χρή.
MH. σὺ δ' ἀλλὰ σὴν κέλευσον αἰτεῖσθαι πάρος—
γυναῖκα παῖδας τήνδε μὴ φεύγειν χθόνα.
IA. μάλιστα, καὶ πείσειν γε δοξάζω σφ' ἐγώ.
MH. εἴπερ γυναικῶν ἐστι τῶν ἄλλων μία.   945
συλλήψομαι δὲ τοῦδέ σοι κἀγὼ πόνου·
πέμψω γὰρ αὐτῇ δῶρ' ἃ καλλιστεύεται
τῶν νῦν ἐν ἀνθρώποισιν, οἶδ' ἐγώ, πολὺ
λεπτόν τε πέπλον καὶ πλόκον χρυσήλατον
παῖδας φέροντας. ἀλλ' ὅσον τάχος χρεὼν   950
κόσμον κομίζειν δεῦρο προσπόλων τινά.
εὐδαιμονήσει δ' οὐχ ἕν, ἀλλὰ μυρία,
ἀνδρός τ' ἀρίστου σοῦ τυχοῦσ' ὁμευνέτου
κεκτημένη τε κόσμον ὅν ποθ' Ἥλιος
πατρὸς πατὴρ δίδωσιν ἐκγόνοισιν οἷς.   955
λάζυσθε φερνὰς τάσδε, παῖδες, ἐς χέρας
καὶ τῇ τυράννῳ μακαρίᾳ νύμφῃ δότε
φέροντες· οὔτοι δῶρα μεμπτὰ δέξεται.
IA. τί δ', ὦ ματαία, τῶνδε σὰς κενοῖς χέρας;
δοκεῖς σπανίζειν δῶμα βασίλειον πέπλων,   960
δοκεῖς δὲ χρυσοῦ; σῷζε, μὴ δίδου τάδε.
εἴπερ γὰρ ἡμᾶς ἀξιοῖ λόγου τινὸς
γυνή, προθήσει χρημάτων, σάφ' οἶδ' ἐγώ.
MH. μή μοι σύ· πείθειν δῶρα καὶ θεοὺς λόγος·
χρυσὸς δὲ κρείσσων μυρίων λόγων βροτοῖς.   965
κείνης ὁ δαίμων, κεῖνα νῦν αὔξει θεός,
νέα τυραννεῖ· τῶν δ' ἐμῶν παίδων φυγὰς

ψυχῆς ἂν ἀλλαξαίμεθ', οὐ χρυσοῦ μόνον.
ἀλλ', ὦ τέκν' εἰσελθόντε πλησίους δόμους
πατρὸς νέαν γυναῖκα, δεσπότιν δ' ἐμήν,   970
ἱκετεύετ', ἐξαιτεῖσθε μὴ φεύγειν χθόνα,
κόσμον διδόντες· τοῦδε γὰρ μάλιστα δεῖ,
ἐς χεῖρ' ἐκείνην δῶρα δέξασθαι τάδε.
ἴθ' ὡς τάχιστα· μητρὶ δ' ὧν ἐρᾷ τυχεῖν
εὐάγγελοι γένοισθε πράξαντες καλῶς.   975
ΧΟ. νῦν ἐλπίδες οὐκέτι μοι παίδων ζόας,   στρ.
οὐκέτι· στείχουσι γὰρ ἐς φόνον ἤδη.
δέξεται νύμφα χρυσέων ἀναδεσμᾶν
δέξεται δύστανος ἄταν·
ξανθᾷ δ' ἀμφὶ κόμᾳ θήσει τὸν "Αιδα   980
κόσμον αὐτὰ χεροῖν.
πείσει χάρις ἀμβρόσιός τ' αὐγὰ πέπλου   ἀντ.
χρυσοτεύκτου τε στεφάνου περιθέσθαι·
νερτέροις δ' ἤδη πάρα νυμφοκομήσει.   985
τοῖον εἰς ἔρκος πεσεῖται
καὶ μοῖραν θανάτου δύστανος· ἄταν δ'
οὐχ ὑπεκφεύξεται.
σὺ δ', ὦ τάλαν, ὦ κακόνυμφε κηδεμὼν τυράννων, στρ. 990
παισὶν οὐ κατειδὼς
ὄλεθρον βιοτᾷ προσάγεις ἀλόχῳ
τε σᾷ στυγερὸν θάνατον.
δύστανε μοίρας, ὅσον παροίχει.   995
μεταστένομαι δὲ σὸν ἄλγος,   ἀντ.
ὦ τάλαινα παίδων
μᾶτερ, ἃ φονεύσεις
τέκνα νυμφιδίων ἕνεκεν λεχέων,
ἅ σοι προλιπὼν ἀνόμως   1000
ἄλλᾳ ξυνοικεῖ πόσις συνεύνῳ.
ΠΑΙ. δέσποιν', ἀφεῖνται παῖδες οἵδε σοὶ φυγῆς,
καὶ δῶρα νύμφη βασιλὶς ἀσμένη χεροῖν
ἐδέξατ'· εἰρήνη δὲ τἀκεῖθεν τέκνοις.
ἔα.
τί συγχυθεῖσ' ἕστηκας ἡνίκ' εὐτυχεῖς   1005
τί σὴν ἔστρεψας ἔμπαλιν παρηίδα
κοὐκ ἀσμένη τόνδ' ἐξ ἐμοῦ δέχει λόγον;
ΜΗ. αἰαῖ.
ΠΑΙ. τάδ' οὐ ξυνῳδὰ τοῖσιν ἐξηγγελμένοις,
ΜΗ. αἰαῖ μάλ' αὖθις. ΠΑΙ. μῶν τιν' ἀγγέλλων τύχην
οὐκ οἶδα, δόξης δ' ἐσφάλην εὐαγγέλου;   1010
ΜΗ. ἤγγειλας οἷ' ἤγγειλας· οὐ σὲ μέμφομαι.
ΠΑΙ. τί δαὶ κατηφεῖς ὄμμα καὶ δακρυρροεῖς;
ΜΗ. πολλή μ' ἀνάγκη, πρέσβυ· ταῦτα γὰρ θεοὶ

κἀγὼ κακῶς φρονοῦσ’ ἐμηχανησάμην.

ΠΑΙ. θάρσει· κάτει τοι καὶ σὺ πρὸς τέκνων ἔτι. 1015

ΜΗ. ἄλλους κατάξω πρόσθεν ἢ τάλαιν’ ἐγώ.

ΠΑΙ. οὔτοι μόνη σὺ σῶν ἀπεζύγης τέκνων·
κούφως φέρειν χρὴ θνητὸν ὄντα συμφοράς.

ΜΗ. δράσω τάδ’. ἀλλὰ βαῖνε δωμάτων ἔσω
καὶ παισὶ πόρσυν’ οἷα χρὴ καθ’ ἡμέραν. 1020
ὦ τέκνα τέκνα, σφῷν μὲν ἔστι δὴ πόλις
καὶ δῶμ’, ἐν ᾧ λιπόντες ἀθλίαν ἐμὲ
οἰκήσετ’ αἰεὶ μητρὸς ἐστερημένοι·
ἐγὼ δ’ ἐς ἄλλην γαῖαν εἶμι δὴ φυγάς,
πρὶν σφῷν ὄνασθαι κἀπιδεῖν εὐδαίμονας, 1025
πρὶν λέκτρα καὶ γυναῖκα καὶ γαμηλίους
εὐνὰς ἀγῆλαι λαμπάδας τ’ ἀνασχεθεῖν.
ὦ δυστάλαινα τῆς ἐμῆς αὐθαδίας.
ἄλλως ἄρ’ ὑμᾶς, ὦ τέκν’, ἐξεθρεψάμην,
ἄλλως δ’ ἐμόχθουν καὶ κατεξάνθην πόνοις, 1030
στερρὰς ἐνεγκοῦσ’ ἐν τόκοις ἀλγηδόνας.
ἦ μήν ποθ’ ἡ δύστηνος εἶχον ἐλπίδας
πολλὰς ἐν ὑμῖν γηροβοσκήσειν τ’ ἐμὲ
καὶ κατθανοῦσαν χερσὶν εὖ περιστελεῖν,
ζηλωτὸν ἀνθρώποισι· νῦν δ’ ὄλωλε δὴ 1035
γλυκεῖα φροντίς. σφῷν γὰρ ἐστερημένη
λυπρὸν διάξω βίοτον ἀλγεινόν τ’ ἐμοί.
ὑμεῖς δὲ μητέρ’ οὐκέτ’ ὄμμασιν φίλοις
ὄψεσθ’, ἐς ἄλλο σχῆμ’ ἀποστάντες βίου.
φεῦ φεῦ· τί προσδέρκεσθέ μ’ ὄμμασιν, τέκνα; 1040
τί προσγελᾶτε τὸν πανύστατον γέλων;
αἰαῖ· τί δράσω; καρδία γὰρ οἴχεται,
γυναῖκες, ὄμμα φαιδρὸν ὡς εἶδον τέκνων.
οὐκ ἂν δυναίμην· χαιρέτω βουλεύματα
τὰ πρόσθεν· ἄξω παῖδας ἐκ γαίας ἐμούς. 1045
τί δεῖ με πατέρα τῶνδε τοῖς τούτων κακοῖς
λυποῦσαν αὐτὴν δὶς τόσα κτᾶσθαι κακά;
οὐ δῆτ’ ἔγωγε. χαιρέτω βουλεύματα.
καίτοι τί πάσχω; βούλομαι γέλωτ’ ὀφλεῖν
ἐχθροὺς μεθεῖσα τοὺς ἐμοὺς ἀζημίους; 1050
τολμητέον τάδ’. ἀλλὰ τῆς ἐμῆς κάκης,
τὸ καὶ προσέσθαι μαλθακοὺς λόγους φρενί.
χωρεῖτε, παῖδες, ἐς δόμους. ὅτῳ δὲ μὴ
θέμις παρεῖναι τοῖς ἐμοῖσι θύμασιν,
αὐτῷ μελήσει· χεῖρα δ’ οὐ διαφθερῶ. 1055
ἆ ἆ.
μὴ δῆτα, θυμέ. μὴ σύ γ’ ἐργάσῃ τάδε·
ἔασον αὐτούς, ὦ τάλαν, φεῖσαι τέκνων,

ἐκεῖ μεθ' ἡμῶν ζῶντες εὐφρανοῦσί με.
μὰ τοὺς παρ' Ἅιδῃ νερτέρους ἀλάστορας,
οὔτοι ποτ' ἔσται τοῦθ' ὅπως ἐχθροῖς ἐγὼ　　　　1060
παῖδας παρήσω τοὺς ἐμοὺς καθυβρίσαι—
πάντως πέπρακται ταῦτα κοὐκ ἐκφεύξεται·
καὶ δὴ 'πὶ κρατὶ στέφανος, ἐν πέπλοισι δὲ　　　　1065
νύμφη τύραννος ὄλλυται, σάφ' οἶδ' ἐγώ.
ἀλλ' εἶμι γὰρ δὴ τλημονεστάτην ὁδόν,
καὶ τούσδε πέμψω τλημονεστέραν ἔτι,
παῖδας προσειπεῖν βούλομαι. δότ', ὦ τέκνα,
δότ' ἀσπάσασθαι μητρὶ δεξιὰν χέρα.　　　　　　1070
ὦ φιλτάτη χείρ, φίλτατον δέ μοι στόμα
καὶ σχῆμα καὶ πρόσωπον εὐγενὲς τέκνων,
εὐδαιμονοῖτον ἀλλ' ἐκεῖ· τὰ δ' ἐνθάδε
πατὴρ ἀφείλετ'. ὦ γλυκεῖα προσβολή,
ὦ μαλθακὸς χρὼς πνεῦμά θ' ἥδιστον τέκνων.　　1075
χωρεῖτε χωρεῖτ'· οὐκέτ' εἰμὶ προσβλέπειν
οἵα τ' ἔθ' ὑμᾶς, ἀλλὰ νικῶμαι κακοῖς.
καὶ μανθάνω μὲν οἷα δρᾶν μέλλω κακά,
θυμὸς δὲ κρείσσων τῶν ἐμῶν βουλευμάτων,
ὅσπερ μεγίστων αἴτιος κακῶν βροτοῖς.　　　　1080

ΧΟ.　πολλάκις ἤδη
διὰ λεπτοτέρων μύθων ἔμολον
καὶ πρὸς ἁμίλλας ἦλθον μείζους
ἢ χρὴ γενεὰν θῆλυν ἐρευνᾶν·
ἀλλὰ γὰρ ἔστιν μοῦσα καὶ ἡμῖν,　　　　　　1085
ἣ προσομιλεῖ σοφίας ἕνεκεν·
πάσαισι μὲν οὔ· παῦρον δὲ, τί μή;
γένος ἐν πολλαῖς εὕροις ἂν ἴσως,
κοὐκ ἀπόμουσον τὸ γυναικῶν·
καί φημι βροτῶν οἵτινές εἰσιν　　　　　　1090
πάμπαν ἄπειροι μηδ' ἐφύτευσαν
παῖδας, προφέρειν εἰς εὐτυχίαν
τῶν γειναμένων.
οἱ μέν τ' ἄτεκνοι, δι' ἀπειροσύνην
εἴθ' ἡδὺ βροτοῖς εἴτ' ἀνιαρὸν　　　　　　1095
παῖδες τελέθουσ' οὐχὶ τεκόντες,
πολλῶν μόχθων ἀπέχονται·
οἷσι δὲ τέκνων ἔστιν ἐν οἴκοις
γλυκερὸν βλάστημ', ὁρῶ μελέτῃ
κατατρυχομένους τὸν ἅπαντα χρόνον,　　　　1100
πρῶτον μὲν ὅπως θρέψουσι καλῶς
βίοτόν θ' ὁπόθεν λείψουσι τέκνοις·
ἔτι δ' ἐκ τούτων εἴτ' ἐπὶ φλαύροις
εἴτ' ἐπὶ χρηστοῖς

μοχθοῦσι, τόδ' ἐστὶν ἄδηλον.
ἐν δὲ τὸ πάντων λοίσθιον ἤδη 1105
πᾶσιν κατερῶ θνητοῖσι κακόν·
καὶ δὴ γὰρ ἅλις βίοτόν θ' ηὖρον
σῶμά τ' ἐς ἥβην ἤλυθε τέκνων
χρηστοί τ' ἐγένοντ'· εἰ δὲ κυρῆσαι,
δαίμων οὗτος φροῦδος ἐς "Αιδην 1110
θάνατος προφέρων σώματα τέκνων.
πῶς οὖν λύει πρὸς τοῖς ἄλλοις
τήνδ' ἔτι λύπην ἀνιαροτάτην
παίδων ἔνεκεν
θνητοῖσι θεοὺς ἐπιβάλλειν; 1115
ΜΗ. φίλαι, πάλαι δὴ προσμένουσα τὴν τύχην
καραδοκῶ τἀκεῖθεν οἷ 'ποβήσεται.
καὶ δὴ δέδορκα τόνδε τῶν Ἰάσονος
στείχοντ' ὀπαδῶν· πνεῦμα δ' ἠρεθισμένον
δείκνυσιν ὥς τι καινὸν ἀγγελεῖ κακόν. 1120

ΑΓΓΕΛΟΣ.

ὦ δεινὸν ἔργον παρανόμως εἰργασμένη,
Μήδεια, φεῦγε φεῦγε, μήτε ναίαν
λιποῦσ' ἀπήνην μήτ' ὄχον πεδοστιβῆ.
ΜΗ. τί δ' ἄξιόν μοι τῆσδε τυγχάνει φυγῆς;
ΑΓΓ. ὄλωλεν ἡ τύραννος ἀρτίως κόρη 1125
Κρέων θ' ὁ φύσας φαρμάκων τῶν σῶν ὕπο.
ΜΗ. κάλλιστον εἶπας μῦθον, ἐν δ' εὐεργέταις
τὸ λοιπὸν ἤδη καὶ φίλοις ἐμοῖς ἔσει.
ΑΓΓ. τί φῄς; φρονεῖς μὲν ὀρθὰ κοὐ μαίνει, γύναι,
ἥτις τυράννων ἑστίαν ᾐκισμένην 1130
χαίρεις κλύουσα κοὐ φοβεῖ τὰ τοιάδε;
ΜΗ. ἔχω τι κἀγὼ τοῖς γε σοῖς ἐναντίον
λόγοισιν εἰπεῖν· ἀλλὰ μὴ σπέρχου, φίλος,
λέξον δ' ὅπως ὤλοντο· δὶς τόσον γὰρ ἂν
τέρψειας ἡμᾶς, εἰ τεθνᾶσι παγκάκως. 1135
ΑΓΓ. ἐπεὶ τέκνων σῶν ἦλθε δίπτυχος γονὴ
σὺν πατρὶ καὶ παρῆλθε νυμφικοὺς δόμους,
ἥσθημεν οἵπερ σοῖς ἐκάμνομεν κακοῖς
δμῶες· δι' οἴκων δ' εὐθὺς ἦν πολὺς λόγος
σὲ καὶ πόσιν σὸν νεῖκος ἐσπεῖσθαι τὸ πρίν. 1140
κυνεῖ δ' ὁ μέν τις χεῖρ', ὁ δὲ ξανθὸν κάρα
παίδων· ἐγὼ δὲ καὐτὸς ἡδονῆς ὕπο
στέγας γυναικῶν σὺν τέκνοις ἅμ' ἑσπόμην.
δέσποινα δ' ἣν νῦν ἀντὶ σοῦ θαυμάζομεν,
πρὶν μὲν τέκνων σῶν εἰσιδεῖν ξυνωρίδα, 1145
πρόθυμον εἶχ' ὀφθαλμὸν εἰς Ἰάσονα·

ἔπειτα μέντοι προυκαλύψατ' ὄμματα
λευκήν τ' ἀπέστρεψ' ἔμπαλιν παρηίδα,
παίδων μυσαχθεῖσ' εἰσόδους· πόσις δὲ σὸς
ὀργάς τ' ἀφήρει καὶ χόλον νεάνιδος   1150
λέγων τάδ'· οὐ μὴ δυσμενὴς ἔσει φίλοις,
παύσει δὲ θυμοῦ καὶ πάλιν στρέψεις κάρα,
φίλους νομίζουσ' οὕσπερ ἂν πόσις σέθεν,
δέξει δὲ δῶρα καὶ παραιτήσει πατρὸς
φυγὰς ἀφεῖναι παισὶ τοῖσδ' ἐμὴν χάριν;   1155
ἡ δ' ὡς ἐσεῖδε κόσμον, οὐκ ἠνέσχετο,
ἀλλ' ᾔνεσ' ἀνδρὶ πάντα, καὶ πρὶν ἐκ δόμων
μακρὰν ἀπεῖναι πατέρα καὶ τέκνα σέθεν,
λαβοῦσα πέπλους ποικίλους ἠμπίσχετο,
χρυσοῦν τε θεῖσα στέφανον ἀμφὶ βοστρύχοις   1160
λαμπρῷ κατόπτρῳ σχηματίζεται κόμην,
ἄψυχον εἰκὼ προσγελῶσα σώματος.
κἄπειτ' ἀναστᾶσ' ἐκ θρόνων διέρχεται
στέγας, ἁβρὸν βαίνουσα παλλεύκῳ ποδί,
δώροις ὑπερχαίρουσα, πολλὰ πολλάκις   1165
τένοντ' ἐς ὀρθὸν ὄμμασι σκοπουμένη.
τοὐνθένδε μέντοι δεινὸν ἦν θέαμ' ἰδεῖν·
χροιὰν γὰρ ἀλλάξασα λεχρία πάλιν
χωρεῖ τρέμουσα κῶλα καὶ μόλις φθάνει
θρόνοισιν ἐμπεσοῦσα μὴ χαμαὶ πεσεῖν.   1170
καί τις γεραιὰ προσπόλων δόξασά που
ἢ Πανὸς ὀργὰς ἤ τινος θεῶν μολεῖν
ἀνωλόλυξε, πρίν γ' ὁρᾷ διὰ στόμα
χωροῦντα λευκὸν ἀφρόν, ὀμμάτων τ' ἄνω
κόρας στρέφουσαν, αἷμά τ' οὐκ ἐνὸν χροΐ·   1175
εἶτ' ἀντίμολπον ἧκεν ὀλολυγῆς μέγαν
κωκυτόν. εὐθὺς δ' ἡ μὲν ἐς πατρὸς δόμους
ὥρμησεν, ἡ δὲ πρὸς τὸν ἀρτίως πόσιν,
φράσουσα νύμφης συμφοράς· ἅπασα δὲ
στέγη πυκνοῖσιν ἐκτύπει δρομήμασιν.   1180
ἤδη δ' ἀνακλῶν κῶλον ἐκπλέθρου δρόμου
ταχὺς βαδιστὴς τερμόνων ἂν ἥπτετο,
ἡ δ' ἐξ ἀναύγου καὶ μύσαντος ὄμματος   1183
δεινὸν στενάξασ' ἡ τάλαιν' ἀνωμμάτου.
διπλοῦν γὰρ αὐτῇ πῆμ' ἐπεστρατεύετο·   1185
χρυσοῦς μὲν ἀμφὶ κρατὶ κείμενος πλόκος
θαυμαστὸν ἵει νᾶμα παμφάγου πυρός·
πέπλοι δὲ λεπτοί, σῶν τέκνων δωρήματα,
λευκὴν ἔδαπτον σάρκα τῆς δυσδαίμονος.
φεύγει δ' ἀναστᾶσ' ἐκ θρόνων πυρουμένη,   1190
σείουσα χαίτην κρᾶτά τ' ἄλλοτ' ἄλλοσε,
ῥῖψαι θέλουσα στέφανον· ἀλλ' ἀραρότως

σύνδεσμα χρυσὸς εἶχε, πῦρ δ', ἐπεὶ κόμην
ἔσεισε, μᾶλλον δὶς τόσως ἐλάπτετο.
πίτνει δ' ἐς οὖδας συμφορᾷ νικωμένη,   1195
πλὴν τῷ τεκόντι κάρτα δυσμαθὴς ἰδεῖν·
οὔτ' ὀμμάτων γὰρ δῆλος ἦν κατάστασις
οὔτ' εὐφυὲς πρόσωπον, αἷμα δ' ἐξ ἄκρου
ἔσταζε κρατὸς συμπεφυρμένον πυρί,
σάρκες δ' ἀπ' ὀστέων ὥστε πεύκινον δάκρυ   1200
γναθμοῖς ἀδήλοις φαρμάκων ἀπέρρεον,
δεινὸν θέαμα· πᾶσι δ' ἦν φόβος θιγεῖν
νεκροῦ· τύχην γὰρ εἴχομεν διδάσκαλον.
πατὴρ δ' ὁ τλήμων συμφορᾶς ἀγνωσίᾳ
ἄφνω παρελθὼν δῶμα προσπίτνει νεκρῷ·   1205
ᾤμωξε δ' εὐθύς, καὶ περιπτύξας χέρας
κυνεῖ προσαυδῶν τοιάδ'· ὦ δύστηνε παῖ,
τίς σ' ὧδ' ἀτίμως δαιμόνων ἀπώλεσε;
τίς τὸν γέροντα τύμβον ὀρφανὸν σέθεν
τίθησιν; οἴμοι, συνθάνοιμί σοι, τέκνον.   1210
ἐπεὶ δὲ θρήνων καὶ γόων ἐπαύσατο,
χρῄζων γεραιὸν ἐξαναστῆσαι δέμας
προσείχεθ' ὥστε κισσὸς ἔρνεσιν δάφνης
λεπτοῖσι πέπλοις, δεινὰ δ' ἦν παλαίσματα·
ὁ μὲν γὰρ ἤθελ' ἐξαναστῆσαι γόνυ,   1215
ἡ δ' ἀντελάζυτ'. εἰ δὲ πρὸς βίαν ἄγοι,
σάρκας γεραιὰς ἐσπάρασσ' ἀπ' ὀστέων.
χρόνῳ δ' ἀπέσβη καὶ μεθῆχ' ὁ δύσμορος
ψυχήν· κακοῦ γὰρ οὐκέτ' ἦν ὑπέρτερος.
κεῖνται δὲ νεκροὶ παῖς τε καὶ γέρων πατὴρ   1220
πέλας, ποθεινὴ δὴ κλύουσι συμφορά.
καί μοι τὸ μὲν σὸν ἐκποδὼν ἔστω λόγου·
γνώσει γὰρ αὐτὴ ζημίας ἀποστροφήν.
τὰ θνητὰ δ' οὐ νῦν πρῶτον ἡγοῦμαι σκιάν.
οὐδ' ἂν τρέσας εἴποιμι τοὺς σοφοὺς βροτῶν   1225
δοκοῦντας εἶναι καὶ μεριμνητὰς λόγων
τούτους μεγίστην ζημίαν ὀφλισκάνειν.
θνητῶν γὰρ οὐδείς ἐστιν εὐδαίμων ἀνήρ·
ὄλβου δ' ἐπιρρυέντος εὐτυχέστερος
ἄλλου γένοιτ' ἂν ἄλλος, εὐδαίμων δ' ἂν οὔ.   1230
ΧΟ. ἔοιχ' ὁ δαίμων πολλὰ τῇδ' ἐν ἡμέρᾳ
κακὰ ξυνάπτειν ἐνδίκως Ἰάσονι.
ὦ τλῆμον, ὥς σου συμφορὰς οἰκτείρομεν,
κόρη Κρέοντος, ἥτις εἰς Ἅδου πέλας
οἴχει γάμων ἕκατι τῶν Ἰάσονος.   1235
ΜΗ. φίλαι, δέδοκται τοὔργον ὡς τάχιστά μοι
παῖδας κτανούσῃ τῆσδ' ἀφορμᾶσθαι χθονὸς
καὶ μὴ σχολὴν ἄγουσαν ἐκδοῦναι τέκνα

ἄλλῃ φονεῦσαι δυσμενεστέρᾳ χερί.
πάντως σφ' ἀνάγκη κατθανεῖν· ἐπεὶ δὲ χρή, 1240
ἡμεῖς κτενοῦμεν, οἵπερ ἐξεφύσαμεν.
ἀλλ' εἶ' ὁπλίζου, καρδία. τί μέλλομεν;
τί δεινὰ τἀναγκαῖα; μὴ πράσσειν κακόν.
ἄγ', ὦ τάλαινα χεὶρ ἐμή, λαβὲ ξίφος,
λάβ', ἕρπε πρὸς βαλβῖδα λυπηρὰν βίου, 1245
καὶ μὴ κακισθῇς μηδ' ἀναμνησθῇς τέκνων
ὡς φίλταθ', ὡς ἔτικτες· ἀλλὰ τήνδε γε
λαθοῦ βραχεῖαν ἡμέραν παίδων σέθεν,
κἄπειτα θρήνει· καὶ γὰρ εἰ κτενεῖς σφ', ὅμως
φίλοι τ' ἔφυσαν, δυστυχὴς δ' ἐγὼ γυνή. 1250
ΧΟ. ἰὼ Γᾶ τε καὶ παμφαὴς   στρ.
ἀκτὶς Ἀελίου, κατίδετ' ἴδετε τὰν
οὐλομέναν γυναῖκα, πρὶν φοινίαν
τέκνοις προσβαλεῖν χέρ' αὐτοκτόνον·
σᾶς γὰρ ἀπὸ χρυσέας γονᾶς 1255
ἔβλαστεν, θεοῦ δ' αἵματι πίτνειν
φόβος ὑπ' ἀνέρων.
ἀλλά νιν, ὦ φάος διογενές, κάτειρ-
γε κατάπαυσον, ἔξελ' οἴκων φονίαν
τάλαινάν τ' Ἐρινὺν ὑπ' ἀλαστόρων. 1260
μάταν μόχθος ἔρρει τέκνων,   ἀντ.
μάταν γένος φίλιον ἔτεκες, ὦ
κυανεᾶν λιποῦσα Συμπληγάδων
πετρᾶν ἀξενωτάταν ἐσβολάν;
δειλαία, τί σοι φρενῶν βαρὺς 1265
χόλος προσπίτνει καὶ δυσμενὴς
φόνος ἀμείβεται;
χαλεπὰ γὰρ βροτοῖς ὁμογενῆ μιά-
σματ', ἔτι τ' αἰὲν αὐτοφόνταισιν οἷ-
δα θεόθεν πίτνοντ' ἐπὶ δόμοις ἄχη. 1270
ΠΑΙΣ. οἴμοι, τί δράσω; ποῖ φύγω μητρὸς χέρας;
ΠΑΙΣ. οὐκ οἶδ', ἀδελφὲ φίλτατ'· ὀλλύμεσθα γάρ.
ΧΟ. ἀκούεις βοὰν ἀκούεις τέκνων;   στρ.
ἰὼ τλᾶμον, ὦ κακοτυχὲς γύναι.
παρέλθω δόμους; ἀρῆξαι φόνον 1275
δοκεῖ μοι τέκνοις.
ΠΑΙΣ. ναί, πρὸς θεῶν, ἀρῆξατ'· ἐν δέοντι γάρ·
ΠΑΙΣ. ὡς ἐγγὺς ἤδη γ' ἐσμὲν ἀρκύων ξίφους.
ΧΟ. τάλαιν', ὡς ἄρ' ἦσθα πέτρος ἢ σίδα-
ρος, ἅτις τέκνων ὃν ἔτεκες ἔτεκες 1280
ἄροτον αὐτόχειρι μοίρᾳ κτενεῖς.
μίαν δὴ κλύω μίαν τῶν πάρος   ἀντ.
γυναικῶν φίλοις χέρα βαλεῖν τέκνοις,

Ἰνὼ μανεῖσαν ἐκ θεῶν, ὅθ᾽ ἡ Διὸς
δάμαρ νιν ἐξέπεμψε δωμάτων ἄλῃ.
πίτνει δ᾽ ἁ τάλαιν᾽ ἐς ἅλμαν φόνῳ
τέκνων δυσσεβεῖ,
ἀκτῆς ὑπερτείνασα ποντίας πόδα,
δυοῖν τε παίδοιν ξυνθανοῦσ᾽ ἀπόλλυται.
τί δῆτ᾽ οὖν γένοιτ᾽ ἂν ἔτι δεινόν; ὦ 1290
γυναικῶν λέχος πολύπονον, ὅσα δὴ
βροτοῖς ἔρεξας ἤδη κακά.

IA. γυναῖκες, αἳ τῆσδ᾽ ἐγγὺς ἕστατε στέγης,
ἆρ᾽ ἐν δόμοισιν ἡ τὰ δείν᾽ εἰργασμένη
Μήδεια τοῖσδ᾽ ἔτ᾽, ἢ μεθέστηκεν φυγῇ; 1295
δεῖ γάρ νιν ἤτοι γῆς σφε κρυφθῆναι κάτω,
ἢ πτηνὸν ἆραι σῶμ᾽ ἐς αἰθέρος βάθος,
εἰ μὴ τυράννων δώμασιν δώσει δίκην·
πέποιθ᾽ ἀποκτείνασα κοιράνους χθονὸς
ἀθῷος αὐτὴ τῶνδε φεύξεσθαι δόμων; 1300
ἀλλ᾽ οὐ γὰρ αὐτῆς φροντίδ᾽ ὡς τέκνων ἔχω,
κείνην μὲν οὓς ἔδρασεν ἔρξουσιν κακῶς,
ἐμῶν δὲ παίδων ἦλθον ἐκσώσων βίον,
μή μοί τι δράσωσ᾽ οἱ προσήκοντες γένει,
μητρῷον ἐκπράσσοντες ἀνόσιον φόνον. 1305

ΧΟ. ὦ τλῆμον, οὐκ οἶσθ᾽ οἷ κακῶν ἐλήλυθας,
Ἰᾶσον· οὐ γὰρ τούσδ᾽ ἂν ἐφθέγξω λόγους.
IA. τί δ᾽ ἔστιν; ἦ που κἄμ᾽ ἀποκτεῖναι θέλει;
ΧΟ. παῖδες τεθνᾶσι χειρὶ μητρᾴα σέθεν.
IA. οἴμοι τί λέξεις; ὥς μ᾽ ἀπώλεσας, γύναι. 1310
ΧΟ. ὡς οὐκέτ᾽ ὄντων σῶν τέκνων φρόντιζε δή.
IA. ποῦ γάρ νιν ἔκτειν᾽; ἐντὸς ἢ ἔξωθεν δόμων;
ΧΟ. πύλας ἀνοίξας σῶν τέκνων ὄψει φόνον.
IA. χαλᾶτε κλῇδας ὡς τάχιστα, πρόσπολοι,
ἐκλύεθ᾽ ἁρμούς, ὡς ἴδω διπλοῦν κακόν, 1315
τοὺς μὲν θανόντας, τὴν δὲ τίσομαι φόνου.

ΜΗ. τί τάσδε κινεῖς κἀναμοχλεύεις πύλας,
νεκροὺς ἐρευνῶν κἀμὲ τὴν εἰργασμένην;
παῦσαι πόνου τοῦδ᾽. εἰ δ᾽ ἐμοῦ χρείαν ἔχεις,
λέγ᾽, εἴ τι βούλει, χειρὶ δ᾽ οὐ ψαύσεις ποτέ. 1320
τοιόνδ᾽ ὄχημα πατρὸς Ἥλιος πατὴρ
δίδωσιν ἡμῖν, ἔρυμα πολεμίας χερός.

IA. ὦ μῖσος, ὦ μέγιστον ἐχθίστη γύναι
θεοῖς τε κἀμοὶ παντί τ᾽ ἀνθρώπων γένει,
ἥτις τέκνοισι σοῖσιν ἐμβαλεῖν ξίφος 1325
ἔτλης τεκοῦσα κἄμ᾽ ἄπαιδ᾽ ἀπώλεσας·
καὶ ταῦτα δράσασ᾽ ἥλιόν τε προσβλέπεις
καὶ γαῖαν, ἔργον τλᾶσα δυσσεβέστατον.
ὄλοι᾽· ἐγὼ δὲ νῦν φρονῶ, τότ᾽ οὐ φρονῶν,

ὅτ' ἐκ δόμου σε βαρβάρου τ' ἀπὸ χθονὸς   1330
"Ελλην' ἐς οἶκον ἠγόμην, κακὸν μέγα,
πατρός τε καὶ γῆς προδότιν ἥ σ' ἐθρέψατο—
τῶν σῶν ἀλάστορ' εἰς ἔμ' ἔσκηψαν θεοί·
κτανοῦσα γὰρ δὴ σὸν κάσιν παρέστιον,
τὸ καλλίπρῳρον εἰσέβης Ἀργοῦς σκάφος.   1335
ἤρξω μὲν ἐκ τοιῶνδε, νυμφευθεῖσα δὲ
παρ' ἀνδρὶ τῷδε καὶ τεκοῦσά μοι τέκνα,
εὐνῆς ἔκατι καὶ λέχους σφ' ἀπώλεσας.
οὐκ ἔστιν ἥτις τοῦτ' ἂν Ἑλληνὶς γυνὴ
ἔτλη ποθ', ὧν γε πρόσθεν ἠξίουν ἐγὼ   1340
γῆμαί σε, κῆδος ἐχθρὸν ὀλέθριόν τ' ἐμοί,
λέαιναν, οὐ γυναῖκα, τῆς Τυρσηνίδος
Σκύλλης ἔχουσαν ἀγριωτέραν φύσιν.
ἀλλ' οὐ γὰρ ἄν σε μυρίοις ὀνείδεσι
δάκοιμι· τοιόνδ' ἐμπέφυκέ σοι θράσος·   1345
ἔρρ', αἰσχροποιὲ καὶ τέχνην μιαιφόνε.
ἐμοὶ δὲ τὸν ἐμὸν δαίμον' αἰάζειν πάρα,
ὃς οὔτε λέκτρων νεογάμων ὀνήσομαι,
οὐ παῖδας οὓς ἔφυσα κἀξεθρεψάμην
ἔξω προσειπεῖν ζῶντας, ἀλλ' ἀπώλεσα.   1350
ΜΗ. μακρὰν ἂν ἐξέτεινα τοῖσδ' ἐναντίον
λόγοισιν, εἰ μὴ Ζεὺς πατὴρ ἠπίστατο
οἷ' ἐξ ἐμοῦ πέπονθας οἷά τ' εἰργάσω·
σὺ δ' οὐκ ἔμελλες τἄμ' ἀτιμάσας λέχη
τερπνὸν διάξειν βίοτον ἐγγελῶν ἐμοί,   1355
οὐδ' ἡ τύραννος, οὐδ' ὁ σοὶ προσθεὶς γάμους
Κρέων ἀνατὶ τῆσδέ μ' ἐκβαλεῖν χθονός.
πρὸς ταῦτα καὶ λέαιναν, εἰ βούλει, κάλει,
[καὶ Σκύλλαν ἢ Τυρσηνὸν ᾤκησεν πέδον]
τῆς σῆς γὰρ ὡς χρὴ καρδίας ἀνθηψάμην.   1360
ΙΑ.   καὐτή γε λυπεῖ καὶ κακῶν κοινωνὸς εἶ.
ΜΗ. σάφ' ἴσθι· λύει δ' ἄλγος, ἢν σὺ μὴ 'γγελᾷς.
ΙΑ.   ὦ τέκνα, μητρὸς ὡς κακῆς ἐκύρσατε.
ΜΗ. ὦ παῖδες, ὡς ὤλεσθε πατρῴᾳ νόσῳ.
ΙΑ.   οὔτοι νυν ἡμὴ δεξιά σφ' ἀπώλεσεν.   1365
ΜΗ. ἀλλ' ὕβρις οἵ τε σοὶ νεοδμῆτες γάμοι.
ΙΑ.   λέχους σφε κἠξίωσας εἵνεκα κτανεῖν.
ΜΗ. σμικρὸν γυναικὶ πῆμα τοῦτ' εἶναι δοκεῖς;
ΙΑ.   ἥτις γε σώφρων· σοὶ δὲ πάντ' ἐστίν, κακή.
ΜΗ. οἵδ' οὐκέτ' εἰσί· τοῦτο γάρ σε δήξεται.   1370
ΙΑ.   οἵδ' εἰσίν, οἶμαι, σῷ κάρᾳ μιάστορες.
ΜΗ. ἴσασιν ὅστις ἦρξε πημονῆς θεοί.
ΙΑ.   ἴσασι δῆτα σήν γ' ἀπόπτυστον φρένα.
ΜΗ. στύγει· πικρὰν δὲ βάξιν ἐχθαίρω σέθεν.

ΙΑ.   καὶ μὴν ἐγὼ σήν· ῥᾴδιον δ᾽ ἀπαλλαγαί.   1375

ΜΗ.   πῶς οὖν; τί δράσω; κάρτα γὰρ κἀγὼ θέλω.

ΙΑ.   θάψαι νεκρούς μοι τούσδε καὶ κλαῦσαι πάρες.

ΜΗ.   οὐ δῆτ᾽, ἐπεὶ σφᾶς τῇδ᾽ ἐγὼ θάψω χερί,
φέρουσ᾽ ἐς Ἥρας τέμενος Ἀκραίας θεοῦ,
ὡς μή τις αὐτοῦ πολεμίων καθυβρίσῃ,   1380
τύμβους ἀνασπῶν· γῇ δὲ τῇδε Σισύφου
σεμνὴν ἑορτὴν καὶ τέλη προσάψομεν
τὸ λοιπὸν ἀντὶ τοῦδε δυσσεβοῦς φόνου.
αὐτὴ δὲ γαῖαν εἶμι τὴν Ἐρεχθέως,
Αἰγεῖ συνοικήσουσα τῷ Πανδίονος.   1385
σὺ δ᾽, ὥσπερ εἰκός, κατθανεῖ κακὸς κακῶς,
Ἀργοῦς κάρα σὸν λειψάνῳ πεπληγμένος,
πικρὰς τελευτὰς τῶν ἐμῶν γάμων ἰδών.

ΙΑ.   ἀλλά σ᾽ Ἐρινὺς ὀλέσειε τέκνων
φονία τε Δίκη.   1390

ΜΗ.   τίς δὲ κλύει σου θεὸς ἢ δαίμων,
τοῦ ψευδόρκου καὶ ξειναπάτου;

ΙΑ.   φεῦ φεῦ, μυσαρὰ καὶ παιδολέτορ.

ΜΗ.   στεῖχε πρὸς οἴκους καὶ θάπτ᾽ ἄλοχον.

ΙΑ.   στείχω, δισσῶν γ᾽ ἄμορος τέκνων.   1395

ΜΗ.   οὔπω θρηνεῖς· μένε καὶ γῆρας.

ΙΑ.   ὦ τέκνα φίλτατα. ΜΗ. μητρί γε, σοὶ δ᾽ οὔ.

ΙΑ.   κἄπειτ᾽ ἔκανες; ΜΗ. σέ γε πημαίνουσ᾽.

ΙΑ.   ὤμοι, φιλίου χρῄζω στόματος
παίδων ὁ τάλας προσπτύξασθαι.   1400

ΜΗ.   νῦν σφε προσαυδᾷς, νῦν ἀσπάζει,
τότ᾽ ἀπωσάμενος. ΙΑ. δός μοι πρὸς θεῶν
μαλακοῦ χρωτὸς ψαῦσαι τέκνων.

ΜΗ.   οὐκ ἔστι· μάτην ἔπος ἔρριπται.

ΙΑ.   Ζεῦ, τάδ᾽ ἀκούεις ὡς ἀπελαυνόμεθ᾽,   1405
οἷά τε πάσχομεν ἐκ τῆς μυσαρᾶς
καὶ παιδοφόνου τῆσδε λεαίνης;
ἀλλ᾽ ὁπόσον γοῦν πάρα καὶ δύναμαι
τάδε καὶ θρηνῶ κἀπιθεάζω,
μαρτυρόμενος δαίμονας ὥς μοι   1410
τέκν᾽ ἀποκτείνασ᾽ ἀποκωλύεις
ψαῦσαί τε χεροῖν θάψαι τε νεκρούς,
οὓς μήποτ᾽ ἐγὼ φύσας ὄφελον
πρὸς σοῦ φθιμένους ἐπιδέσθαι.

ΧΟ.   πολλῶν ταμίας Ζεὺς ἐν Ὀλύμπῳ,   1415
πολλὰ δ᾽ ἀέλπτως κραίνουσι θεοί·
καὶ τὰ δοκηθέντ᾽ οὐκ ἐτελέσθη,
τῶν δ᾽ ἀδοκήτων πόρον ηὗρε θεός.
τοιόνδ᾽ ἀπέβη τόδε πρᾶγμα.